AENEAS AND SON

VIRGIL'S AENEID 1959

JAMES RUSSELL

Published in the United Kingdom in 2023
by The Knives Forks And Spoons Press,
51 Pipit Avenue,
Newton-le-Willows,
Merseyside,
WA12 9RG.

ISBN 978-1-912211-99-9

Acknowledgements:

The author wishes to acknowledge the inspiration received from reading the fine translation of Virgil's poem by Shadi Bartsch, and her wonderfully useful accompanying text: *The Aeneid: A New Translation*, Profile Books, 2020.

For Paddy

Contents

Aeneas & Son and *The Aeneid*

Something of the spirit of Virgil's poem has been transposed to southern England in 1959. All of the major and most of the minor events and characters are here, the events refracted through modernity or new narratives, the characters thinly disguised (Laocoön is Loud Colin; the harpies are Mrs Harpic; Pallas is Patsy), and the relocations easy to spot (Troy is in Richmond; Carthage is a village in Wiltshire; the games are in Weymouth; the nascent Rome is Bristol). But readers need to know nothing of *The Aeneid* (or even to have heard of it) to enjoy this freewheeling, humorous, and socially reflective verse novel. In an addendum, Virgil's founding myth of the Roman Empire becomes the founding myth of the digital world.

AENEAS AND SON

VIRGIL'S AENEID 1959

One: The Stop-Off

Their song is a threesome song about three men:
Three Cool Cats by the Coasters.
Singing in a Standard Ten on the Great West Road
in 1959, travelling West, their life going south —
or so it seems that night.

My song is about one of the three men —
both a son & a father: Ed or Eddy or Edwin Hale,
nicknamed Hale-&-Farewell.
Handsome, physically powerful; but mentally
a man imprisoned by his own imaginings.
Also & certainly a mummy's man.
Imaginings? When he comes up against
or alongside, below or above persons with a particular
power, manufactured or secreted by him alone, they stamp him
with a mental mark: maybe just an over-sharp
petrol attendant, a shockingly sweet bus conductress —
such that they remain to hover over his mind
with causal powers as real as anvils.
They are beings with whom
he can speak & have his dialogic dramas.

He ascribes to them powers, & because he does
they have real powers willy nilly.

This is an impeding force of course of course
& it is spiked with a dangerous liquor —
superstition. He believes he has the tools on him
(the number three is back) to tell the future:
three coins not in a fountain (the three would
sing this too) but tucked away in an old
schoolboy purse beside a copy of the Chinese

book of divination, the *I Ching.*
He thinks — he really does — that throwing three
coins onto a table six times can foreshadow (it is
mainly shadows) what is to come in his life.

He is buffeted more than most by fate.
But he buffets himself for good measure.
That's the picture.

Maybe El Greco could paint the picture
of his mind right now —
blackest sky, turbulent illumination of spirit-steam,
purple-fringed face in the cloud canopy
her steaming hair melting into the wind-prow.
Her?
Yes, the face of Ioanna — the agent of their home-loss
& overseeing devil of the flight West.

More, much more, of Ioanna later — the historical her,
the real meat and poison of her; but for now the mental
of her is doing all the work in the Ed-mentality.

As for the car, this is the focus of his fear. He lives
in a fever of car threats, even the wondering why
Standard Tens are nearly always lavatory green.
The motor (a 1952) was bought for cash on an oily
forecourt in Brentford, the cool cats having tramped
across Kew Bridge in extremis a few days earlier.
& Eddy was convinced, he was bloody *positive,*

that he'd seen Ionanna's son Stelios
chatting to the camel-hair-coated spiv who'd done them
a favour ('I'm cutting me own throat here mate') by selling
it to them. The camel had said he'd throw in a service
'gratis and for nothing' but this was *after* the chat to
the geezer who could bloody-well have been Stelios.

Some service this. A service that makes the steering pull
to the off-side — he's *positive* it does —
& this spoiled his spasm of delight
when an AA motorbike-and sidecar rider saluted
him on seeing the yellow badge on the motor's bonnet,
not remotely like a daffodil on a lawn.

& are there not flat spots
when he puts his foot down & a sponginess
on breaking?
& is not the engine 'missing' now & then?
A stuttering progress — he's definite —
a timing problem was in there for certain sure.
It has to be said that
the long reach of Ioanna is toying
with his small intestine. He feels
too they should consider their money stash.
Did he not leave the duffle bag unattended
(attended only by his son that is) when he
went for a slash in the caff near the garage?

But these demons all live behind the mask
of Ed's bland regard. The other two know
he sneaks off to throw coins to question the oracle.
They know he is ever vigilant
for phone boxes so he can ring his mum (so distant
& yet with a reach not only as long as Ioanna's but
within the *physical* realm that Ed thinks of
as a holiday island clear of his mental storms); but they
know nothing of the Ed's inner furies
that hover always. They tease him
about the coins and call boxes each in his own way:
his dad dry and sly from the corner of the mouth;
his son like a ten-year-old coming down
from a sugar rush. Now a word

or two about them …
In the passenger seat is his dad — Leslie (or Les).
He's a dangerous, interesting walnut.
In the back seat is his son — another Edwin
but Ned (not Ed).
Ned's a seal, smooth with hard blubber
from eating, sloth, & binding agents:
imagine a cream-coloured aubergine.
Not very interesting (on the surface). Likeable.

While Les lives in pubs & in back-rooms with card tables
he has the tan of a building-site toiler, a face as kippered
as his smoker's lungs must be, lined as a thought-
wracked philosopher; & the twinkling eyes of
a man with a past.
Here is an element of that past
that's right to the point. During

the final years of the first world war, years in London
of gaiety, despite & because of the steady slaughter overseas,
he was swimming in his element.
The phrase 'a ladies' man' was alive and well
in the teen years of the 20th century; it was almost
his occupation. This snatch of an otherwise filthy ditty
from the second world war comes to mind:

I'd rather hang around Piccadilly Underground
Living off the earnings of a high-born lady

In those days he was a handsome, dashing liar.
In Mayfair bars, in his only suit, he would
flirt & flirt & spin yarns about the top-secret missions
the government had sent him on, dripping more
baloney about the sexual peccadillos of the 'high-ups'.

One of his conquests was debutante Lady Vera de Vere
McInnes, her name often changing since with new husbands

& their newly-acquired titles. To us she'll just be
Lady Vera or just Vera.
Les (under the name
of Jack Hawksmore) swept her off her feet as a
necessary condition to impregnating her.
She was rushed off to Inverness where she
gave birth to Edwin.
She could not bear
to be parted from the lovely mite
& decided that Les would bring him up
so she could hover near.
His pay-off was huge, as were the subsequent
gambling losses & bar bills & hotel charges. Her
plan was that that Edwin would remain in her life.
He did & does.

Vera's houses are dotted all over this island,
so her hearths are never far from him. While those
she calls 'my gals and chaps' act as her
representing bodies & meet to advise him
on this and that. He & his mother rarely
meet & only in badly-lit loci.
He feels — he really does feel —
that when he meets a gal or a chap he is
meeting her. That's how it feels &
that's what counts, for the time being.

Meanwhile, his counteracting of the offside pulling
persuaded the motor off the Great West Road
South-Westwards. Ed feels that a left turn
to Newbury is more in-keeping with the car's
acquired personality than a tugging right-on
to Swindon. Ned sleeps

& Les perks up at the 'nice-looking boozers
around here' as they edge through Newbury
on to the A343 towards Andover. Suddenly

Ned is awake with a heartfelt whinge:
"I'm staaaarving. Can't we stop for summat daaaad?"
"I'm with the lad," said Les decisively.

Their parked motor is dwarfed by lorries
en route to Southampton; & steam and a jukebox
are the main motifs in the welcome transport caff.
Plus, of course, the aromas and sounds of frying.
While Les makes do with beans on toast and a couple
of *Senior Service,* Ned gets outside of sausage, egg,
chips & beans — chased down by two individual fruit pies.
For Ed, fried bread & tinned tomatoes & a pork pie.
Sweet tea's the main tipple; two milky *Camp* coffees
for Ned & a *Mars Bar.*

It's getting late & the place is
thinning out —
drivers getting back on the road or going off to sleep
in their cabs.
"We'll kip in the car," says Ed.
"Not sure I fancy that," said Les.

He (being Les) is fancying something else, however.
Dream Lover, a recent Bobby Darin hit
is a frequent visitor to the juke box & swaying
to it by the juke box is the object of his gaze —
late 40s, heavily made-up, high-heeled, red-headed
and seemingly alone.   Les (being Les)
quickly dons his suit jacket because it has
padded shoulders from which he benefits.
        Yes, in passing, he wears a suit that is,
like Les, of indeterminate age: chocolate brown, double-
breasted, with wide chalk-stripes. & in passing, again,
Ed is a suit-wearer too, but in a quite different way:
"Italian" in style with narrow lapels and trousers,
bum-freezer jacket. Yes, a little short in the leg,

to highlight his beige socks; &, yes, short
in the arm too (fray of cuff). He seems to be bursting
out of it like a wartime sausage.

"You'd better not be paying for this dad. Remember
what happened last time," says Ed.
"S'fine Eddy. It'll only cost me a couple of Babycham
& brandies. Boozer over the road. Wish me luck."

How old is Les?
We only know that he's mortal.

& that he has a sweet singing voice. He pushes in
a shilling for five more selections, standing next to her,
accompanying Darin.

"Get you!"

"Care to waltz?" A Sinatra disc has just come on.
Now, surely, Ed didn't hear him say a little later:
"Must go for a slash. Don't go away doll."
He stops off at the table of his kin …
"She got a caravan not far away. See you
in the morning fellas."   Whatever Les
has had not skipped a generation. Ed looks
at his smiling, sated son as the lad is half-
deciding to try
a hand-jive to a Helen Shapiro number.
            But Ned has the better of it in the night,
stretching out in the back of the motor.
Ed barely sleeps in the awkward billet of the driver's seat,
& cold too; eventually he folds Les' overcoat
over the steering wheel for a pillow & drifts into
of a fitful sleep thinking of the welcoming call-box
yards away & his dad snugly in his element
in the rocking caravan.

"Look sharp! Her husband works nights." Is what Les
says as he bangs on the window at 6.30.

"Look sharp yourself. I'm phoning mum for advice."
Ed puts his overcoat over his head and heads
for the call box.

"Dahrling! I was worried about you." She knows
all about their homeless & westward-bound state.
"So, it's just you, the old ram, and Neddy Diddums …
Heavens! So, what can I do for you?"

"Well … the *Ching* tells me to head west to plant
a brilliant future, or words to that effect."

The *I Ching* habit he had inherited from Lady Vera herself.
It was the legacy of her liaison with a friend
of Mr Teazy Weazy, a kind of soothsaying shyster
& charm monger called Vadim Leong. She thinks now
it's all nonsense but it hooks on
to something in Ed. & not only because questions like
'What is my future in the West Country?' are answered
with un-nuanced sun-bursts of splendour (while much else
is a contradictory mish-mash quite beyond him).

Yet, for some reason, Vera is all for the Western push.

"Oh, I'm sure that's right dahrling … press on … go west
young man and all that jazz … press on."

"But where to and what to do … mum?"

"I'll tell you what … " He knows what's coming up.

"Where are you?"

"Just outside Andover on the A3— "

"Yes, yes. But what jolly good fortune. You're not
so far from the Salisbury Cromer-Puselys; & one of my
gals looks after their stables. Look. I'll tell her to
meet you at 10.30 in the nearest Wimpy Bar to
the Market Square in Andover. There's bound to be one of each …
But look, how *are* you dahrling? Are you eating properly?"

"Oh yes. Last night I had fried —

"Yes, yes, of course you did dahrling. Must dash though.
Appalling thing is I have an appointment at the hair-dressers.
The gal's name's Marie.
Ciao precious-boots."

As ever, after a call to her, he feels both warmed
and frozen to the quick at once, cuddled up and punched.
He catches sight of himself in the caff-window:
his face a morass of lumbering puzzlement.

"Andover! Ooo how delaightful."
After an Ed-Vera call Les must affect posh.
"One's always wanted to visit
that quait naice plaice."

"Why we goin' a Hanover?" (Ned)

"I've got to meet somebody in a Wimpy Bar."

"Oh, how droll. Edwin and maiself will discharge
our hungers in a cafeteria or horse trough … good enough
for the laiks of us."

Is she (Marie) wearing jodhpurs — the strapping Marie?
Or do her buttocks or hips naturally flare that way?
He wouldn't mind finding out.
He's spent the best part of half an hour
scratching dried ketchup from the nozzle of a plastic tomato

& eating a rum baba. So here she is.
While all her gals varied from A to Z they were
all the same — somehow not present
& yet emphatically who they are.

The whole Wimpy can hear her:
"Oh, it's such a shock when one actually
encounters coffee beneath the froth."

He forces a laugh.

"You look done-in old chap. Buck up!"
She grasps one of his shoulders pushing
and pulling as if to reactivate a toy or stalled donkey.
"Anyway, I've been asking around. Keep on
in this general direction but take the A3086
& stop at a delightful village called Shrewton.
You will find there a charming white-washed hostelry
name of *The Catherine Wheel*; not to be confused
with a *Waggon Wheel*, the big
bouncing biscuit of that name. Ha-ha."

"Ha-Ha"

"Lady Vera is minded that you need
a sympathetic ear and a sojourn in soft sheets
& bready, herby, ointmenty aromas."

He wishes dad was present to hear this.

She fills in background, skewering him
with her rod-like regard: "The proprietress
of *The Wheel* is just like you Edwin: a refugee,
a homeless soul swirled and swished around
like a sock in the proverbial washing machine."

He perks up at this.

"Oh, granted, she has settled status as Mine Hostess,
small-holdings, is indeed a community pillar & fixed
beacon. But, spiritually her home is in far Shaftesbury —
from which she was so cruelly uprooted ten years ago."

"Tell me more, please." (Bored, he could fancy a Wimpy
& chips.)

"Her husband Sean Gillespie —
she is by the way Mrs Dana Gillespie —
was in business with her brother Roy 'Piggy'
Palfrey. Their business was that of 'home improvements'.
It thrived, & their coffers were brimming over.
That it thrived was due to their being, well,
criminals. And here I must pause to release a laugh.
Their chutzpah dahrling, their brass cheek and
neck. Oh dear, oh very dear … "

'Yes, ha-ha." Yes, they are jodhpurs he decides.

She collects herself. "While performing these
'improvements' (some shelving, shower installing)
they would find out how best the home might
be burgled (key under which flowerpot, which
sash is lift-able) then tip off burglar colleagues & share
the spoils. Their burglar friends would lay false evidence
of forced entry, replace keys under mats etc.
All well and good."

"I suppose."

"Now, Piggy Palfrey is not a nice man. Piggy
is a nasty little shit, pardon-my-French. He did
this: he went to the police and spun a yarn that
Sean, the hubby, was doing this solo & with his ignorance
of what they were up to in tandem. He'd planned it
as a long game, planting evidence, burning documents;

and as the police were collaring Sean he withdrew
all the gold from their coffers. Sean could not stop him.
Meanwhile Dana stumbles upon the truth — "

A snort from Ed.

"Oh, don't be like that Edwin. She's as true as a diamond,
a real oyster, a trouper, an upright nun of a girl guide —
compared to her pig-brother and shady worst-half.
Piggy gave a her a big slice of his 'winnings' to keep her gob shut.
She shifted East to Shrewton & bought *The Wheel* &
developed interests in other ventures. Sean released from clink.
She writes to him forgivingly; he writes back on the theme of
blood being thicker than water and said *Awah wee ye bonnie lassie*."

"Is he Scottish?"

"From Taunton … SILLY!!! Now Sean is dead to her. Piggy too.
Her fixture at *The Wheel* is real enough but feels to her
like a false thing in a web of strangers. She herself, I say,
is nurturing, faithful, a paragon. A blonde."

"Natural blonde?"

Now Marie is convulsed with laughter. The whole Wimpy
seems to explode with it. It shudders. Suddenly as it settles
she kisses him on both cheeks and shoots off as if she had never
been there, leaving Ed to order a cola and ponder
the wobbly status of a Vera gal.   Like all the gals
she reminds him of his dear mother, of what he can retain
of her from shadowed meetings in dive bars & snooker halls
& the faded images of childhood. The mannerisms:
the sudden jutting of the chin for emphasis, the strange
sprinkling gesture as if to rid the hand of something
sticky (wet dough, say) when being vague, the random
emphasis on syllables, & the mix of hard addressee-
focus and utter indifference.

More indifference (overt, articulate) from the other two
when he finds them sheltering under a tree in the Market Square,
when he tells them of the Shrewton plan.
"So, what do you suggest we do instead?"
"Wait in the car till the pubs open." (Les)
"Dunno. Go home … Oh." (Ned)
Of course, being Ed, the first thing he'd done
after Marie vanished was to consult the oracle about the plan.
He could have taken the *Woman's Own* he'd found on a seat
and thrown his coins on that as he sat in the stall of the gents;
but he opted for a surreptitious, one-handed job at his table
which was well clear of other patrons (as Marie's volume
has persuaded them away). This would stretch
his short-term memory (he had no pen and paper)
but it was well trained from long experience in the *Ching* domain.

The oracle's response? Ambiguous, giving with one hand etc. —
more grist for grumbling:
the immediate future would be a time of 'peace' & sweet-
hearted glory, but the top line told him something about the walls
of the castle crumbling into the moat & Do Not Act.
No, he would not act. He would soak up the comfort & joy
& let things happen to him. Why aspire
to agency?

The trouble is that to be an agent you need self-desired goals.
You need that throbbing box of start-ups & he really has only two goals:

(1) to have back his happy past

(2) to find a home that is as homely as the home
he's left.

This western move looks unpromising.
He'd half-expected some brightening & softening,
something new but unchallenging;
but he is finding only a more spacious

& weakened version of all the familiar avoidables.
He liked Londony London, where you wake
to the quiet roar of city life. He liked the land west
of West London where the river winds through green banks
laying little islands, not London, no, but nicely near it.

They are quiet as they drive, with Ed's mind stuck
again on his *certainty* that something Ioanna-inspired
is up with the motor.
"She keeps missing" fell from his lips.
"Don't be soft" fell from his dad's.
"I just need to adjust the tappets, clean the plugs."
"Don't be a berk."
"I'll pull over."
"Don't be a berk dad."
"Watch it, Ned!"

The rain is hammering hard & his mind is truly stuck —
and that's that.   He fumbles
in the glove compartment for his tappet-gauge. Regardless
of the rain he goes outside & lifts the bonnet,
unconscious of the fact that they are now in Shrewton,
blinkered from the whitewashed, thatched cottages, & from
the river Till trickling flowing neatly
between them and the High Street
because the Thames between Kingston and Kew
is flowing though his thoughts.

"That's fixed her." They start off & at first all is well.
"There!"
"It was fine before. Just hope you didn't get rain on the plugs …
For fuck's — "
The motor pauses & leaps, pauses & leaps, as if stopping
to think then suddenly remembering what it is about.
It reminded Les, in his woman-centred frame, of a gamine actress
playfully being a sex kitten, foreshadowing Cat Woman.
He laughs hard. Ed swears hard &

the car stops.
Stops about 30 yards from *The Catherine Wheel.*
Ed tells his dad to steer while he and Ned push.
Strong pushers, they over-shoot the target.
"Get in & brake dad!" as they sail past the pub.

This is Dana's first view of her soon-to-be lover:
a large rain-soaked muscular arse straining
through navy-blue cheap suiting, hint of exposed arse-
crack, tiny jacket hitched
up near the armpits, trouser bottoms hitched up
over the calves, muddy beige socks.   Marie
has telephoned (her net as wide as Vera's) earlier
& Dana has been watching the rain & waiting.

The word 'London' spurs in her the adrenalin of adventure
& all that
this pretty place falls short of. Here is a London man.
To leave London on a western quest makes him a kind
of hero, albeit a barely intelligible one. She grabs
an umbrella and runs outside.

"What rotten luck — "

"Not bad *luck* darlin' [Les]. I'd told him to leave — "

"Oh, you must be granddad."

That one word strangles in its cradle his routine erotic charge.
& the final twist of the wrist comes when he has to watch
as Dana makes a beeline for Ned, touches his arm saying
"You're soaking!"
"Not as soaking as our dad, Miss."

She ignores Ed, taking Ned under her wing …
"Come in all of you. I'm just about to open the bar … I say,
are you old enough to drink?"

"Not half. Shandy, sweet cider, stuff of that kind.
Just the job, Miss."

Les & Ed sit now with their pints in the ancient dark of the public bar,
feeling pleasantly alien among the oak & brass.

All she has said to Ed up to this point is a slow & low 'Hello',
looking straight into his eyes
while slightly widening her own.
He's got the message.
So Ed, unlike his dad, can enjoy the weird
process of her evoking from Ned their adventures so far,
which on his telling, were one aborted meal after another
while dashing randomly from billet to pointless billet, all
as breathless as a Tom & Jerry cartoon.

"You're in luck [Dana speaks]. I've got two vacant rooms at present.
One with twin beds and one double."

"Fine," says Ed, smiling slowly and with a twinkle that has not been
in evidence for months, "twin beds for Granddad & Neddy then."

"Thank God," she thinks and it shines on her face: not only
does he get the point, but he has a sense of humour.

Her first sight of him has not lifted her heart.
But, when he'd turned from pushing, the promise was fulfilled.
A muscular presence. Serious. Muscularly tugging down
his bum-freezer & its sleeves, tugging down the trouser bottoms
below his calves, correcting his hair.

His hair!
His hair was un-Brylcreemed, unquiffed, not
combed back, but parted at the side
with the parting amplified by a straight blow-wave
in a style favoured by playboys, as she has seen
in her *Daily Mirror*. The dark hair is

a similar short length all over. Playboys, yes.
That is it!
He evokes for her …
Francisco 'Baby' Pignatari
pioneer of what would become Eurotrash, King
of the European playboys.
But Baby Pignatari as interpreted by a hod-carrier.
No, not.
He is *not* absurd. He is touching. So touching
she could weep with lustful relief
at his winkle-pickers which lace at the sides.
At-the-side is his motif; & she is at his side.

Edwin 'Baby' Hale —
Yes. But there is strength there, the robust calm
of a pious family man.
Of course
she would not think it like that
& neither would she think it like this,
but this is thought:
'Baby' Hale — here is somebody whose reach
exceeds his grasp by a mile, but what a reach,
a heroic reach
& all in the right direction.

Yes, this is a familiar madness, as if the potent fluence
of two hovering spirits had combined to
wash her downstream to the weir of this dependency.
                    But right now she's riding the wave
of his presence
as two of the three (the two who'd slept little last night
for different reasons) are struggling under the hoppy cloud
of the local brew they've drunk with their lunch of bread & cheese
& home-made pickled onions.

"Tell you what," says Les, "do you mind if I nip up
for a spot of shut-eye. Uh … wind kept me awake last night."

"Me too, I'm afraid," says Ed.
Dana's hard disappointed look
follows him out of the bar.

Now Ned is even more excited & suggests that Dana joins him in a game of cards. She explains that she has to serve customers.

"Not even three-card brag Miss. I can help with the serving — "

"Why not go for a walk around. Maybe get the bus up to Stonehenge."

"Stone … HENGE!" He's beside himself.

Three hours later Ed is up and refreshed, meets Dana on the stairs.

"Lock-in tonight," she tells him with some embarrassment.
He wonders if this is local slang
for something exciting and secret they can share.
It's explained how a *Catherine Wheel* lock-in involves
not only the bar staying open after the pub's closed
& the doors locked (no care: police aware)
but a 'feast' in which lock-in-ees pay 7/6^{d} a head.
But she'll wave the charge " … as it's you … three [blushing].
& you can be guest of honour [blushing]."

"Bang on! I'm off for a walk."

The sun's out now. It's as if a film that had started
in harsh black & white is now in pale dreamy colour —
from *Battleship Potemkin* to *Genevieve* say.
He loves it, but is losing his grip on who is doing
the loving. It's all too neat — the village, the circumstance:

from the mallards on the trickling River Till
to the perfectly crunchy pickles,
the pretty & willing Dana.
& why does he feel so exposed beneath this wide sky?
It's not as if anybody could be watching. But for him
it *is* as if somebody is watching — Ioanna, Vera …
The abstract nouns that form the currency of the normal mind
are people in his mind, concrete and immaterial (I'll say no
more on this … probably).

That said, his mind is lighter now he can feel the sunny side,
finds himself wanting to tarry & get his fill, as he wanders back
to the pub. So, he's more amused than embarrassed
by his son's predictable fever of generosity.
Ned had been in the boot of the motor, extracted
what he thought to be the most proud objects
from their previous household
& presented them to Dana: a tiny brass head of Nefertiti
(he said "Cleopatra") loosely attached to a chipped wooden base,
an ashtray in the form of a skull into which you can insert
a smoking cigarette, bearing the motto: "Better to smoke
here than hereafter."
        Ned has no idea what this means but he laughs long
and nudges her in a 'geddit?' manner.

"Oh, how lovely of you," says Dana. "I really think it's
inspiring me to take up smoking."

Also predictable is the evening in the pub, pre-lock-in.
Les is forever just falling short of being a public nuisance
with women who seem unattached but aren't; all bar one —
who strings him along watched by her mates.
        While Ned, emboldened by one lager & lime, goes
to sit near some old men playing dominos, hoping to
learn how to play & fetching them pints when told
so to do.

Mostly alone, Ed watches Dana & is impressed.
Her unattractive desperation to please is gone.
She is naturally the boss & can banter with an edge,
give orders to her staff with a firm familiar ease.
He catches the difference between her almost unaccented
speech & the low oo-ahr mumble of the regulars. She's
slightly and rightly impatient with the patronising upper-crust
couples there. Easy to spot: male in blazer & cavalry twills, cravat;
female in silk headscarf & slacks plus maybe a cigarette-holder.
These all stay for the lock-in, handing over their $7/6^d$s-
often as 10/- notes and a breezy "Keep the change.
Have one on us;" unless it's Dana herself.

The lights are dimmed, the doors locked; Dana tunes in a large walnut
wireless to Radio Luxembourg & the promise of the cooking
aromas is revealed.
Here come chicken pieces fresh from the oven, hot
sausage rolls, a sliced veal & ham pie, cheese (choice
of cheddar, 'Dutch', & *Dairylea* triangles), bread rolls,
more of these supreme pickled onions & pickled cabbage
spilling over the dish like ripped and chopped small intestines,
& a large pat of pale, unshaped farmhouse butter.

Ed marvells at how the patronising poshos tuck in
no less fiercely than Ned, aiming it seems
for $12/6^d$ worth of nutrient. The viands vanished
like frost under sun; people grow quieter; 'shorts'
are being drunk; a posho couple begins to dance
with a kind of defiance that caused coolness from
the worker constituents, dance to a Edmund Hockridge
ballad that David Jacobs has just spun. Some folks drift home
(work the next day), as another posho couple begins to
gaze rudely hard at Ed, who looks out of place because
he is destined so to look & because of the tension
between the way his suit evokes Norman Wisdom &
the way his physical presence evokes an oak planted
by a stream.

"I say," says the woman, "do you mind my asking whereabouts
in London you hail from?"

"No, I don't mind." Ed has just drained the large brandy
Dana has just brought him & he's feeling cocky.

"Where ARE you from?" This from the almost-angry husband.

"Richmond-upon-Thames."

They looked as if their feet had just touched the bottom after
an exhausting swim to shore.

"Oh reeeilleh!" says the man.

"We know people there, how Interesting —" begins the woman.

At once, Dana comes over.

"Neddy tells me that you had quite a time of it.
Seems you didn't exactly leave there by choice.
Neddy said something about you being 'convicted
for woodworm' or something."

"Ees been convicted for woodworm Trev" (one of the domino men)
Much laughter.

Dana rides over it: "Can you tell us more?"

He feels free to talk as the other two have turned in.
Both posho couples sit themselves eagerly near, the oo-ahrr mumblers
mutter and snigger a little as he begins.

Two: Bubbles

There are people who speak quietly knowing
others will strain their ears to hear them;
some speak quietly because for them speaking aloud
is a form of talking to oneself; & some, like Ed,
speak quietly — do on occasions — as a cry
for release from the underground dungeon
of having to speak at all.

This afternoon was the first time ever (give or take)
he has slept alone in a *double* bed. It is a bliss
he wants & wants now. He is not tired.
He wants to spread his arms and legs onto
cool dark solitude, and reflect. Who are these yokels
& poshos, this weirdly available blonde; & all tucked
inside a biscuit-tin village?
But as we shall see,
he will warm up to a sturdy volume & all
without the help of much-proffered drink.

So, when he begins it's as something metamorphosed
only a few notches east of the ooh-ahrr mumbles around him.
He articulates, but implicitly, & as if passing on a racing tip
near a suspicious copper.

To an ear unused to him, something like this is
heard at first:

"Tell you nothing, the kin bubbles did for us."

Blazerred man: "Didn't catch that old boy.
What's a kin bubble?"

Stung into life by this Ed says:

"So sorry Claude — "

"Actually, my name's Dirk — "

"So sorry Claude, what I said was:
I will tell you for nothing that the FU-
cking bubbles did for us."

The audience looks as if it has collectively been slapped
hard across the face so Dana cuts in reasonably with:

"Bubbles, Ed?"

"Rhyming slang darlin'. Bubble & Squeak — Greek.
The Greeks of Richmond. Miss Ioanna Panagiotidou, especially,
& her family of greasy Greeks & their olive-oily pals … "

At this point of discomfort, when there is shifting in seats
beneath an atmosphere of thunderhead, the floor passes entirely
to Edwin (in my telling) — unless there are the discourses of others
explicitly marked.

Yeah, when I went next door and saw dad had
put his foot through the bloody floor, saw
the wood-wormy boards & that sodding horse —
I mean the wooden clothes horse — in the corner
I knew the tenancy rules, right? Didn't I though?
I've not had much of an education, but I'm not thick, okay?
If they find you've 'distressed the fabric' of your 'unit'
then you 'fall under investigation' & I'm cute enough
to know that this would lift the stone we'd managed to like
hide under nice & cosy.
    The tenancy tenure couldn't stand too much investigation
& it was done all thanks to Ioanna & those bubbles.
I'll get to that though. Time for a top-up maybe.
    Ta!   I'll back off a bit.

We've lived all over the shop. Going
where the work is.
Dad was on the busses for a bit,
rag & bone, odd jobs; I'm on building sites mainly, helping out
in pubs needing a bit of muscle, removals; after he left school
Ned did park work, grave-digging, paper sacks
on a Saturday morning.

"And Ned's mum? Just curious" says Dana.

Oh Eunice. Housewife of course. Cook & clean for us.
Barmaid, yeah. Cleaning in some big houses.

But then in this Mortlake pub when Dad — Les —
was a night-watchman at the brewery he meets
this geezer who tells him about these things
called Alms Houses. Says how there are some
not so far away in Richmond. Not right in the centre:
on the road out to East Sheen. Great
little billets, almost no rent, charity jobs more or less
& of course you got to be eligible. So, dad gets the idea
off this geezer that with a bit of touching up here & there,
a bit of gilding the old lily & what did he say?
'digging some special potatoes from a dubious trench or two' —

"Whaaat?" (a domino man)

Dad could sort of make himself eligible like. & more than this,
now this is sweet, we could 'make the case' he says for me
Eunice, & Ned to live there too to 'support' poor old dad
(*laughs hard*).

Cut a long story short, it worked, didn't it?
& we ends up in the bloody fantastic palace of a place
compared to what we're used to. I kid you not,
it was like living in a castle.
It was like living in one of them Oxford & Cambridge colleges:

all little billets round a quadrangle, all grey stone & nooks
where you could bump into a gargoyle or a statue
of a god or of some ancient bint.   No,
it was like one of these training places the church runs
where they train up blokes to be vicars, set back
from the road, little world of its own, like it wasn't
next door to the South Circular at all but was like
in some little market town   or
a place like this, come to think of it.

Then there was us living in Richmond among
the richees. It's not London, not even *like* London;
but it's at the end of the District Line &
on the railway between Reading & Waterloo.
Don't yawn! That's my job. (*laughs*)
Toy Town, that's what it is; though without
Desmond the Dachshund, Larry the Lamb,
& The Mayor.
Mister Mayor says: 'I've breeved on those cream buns
so you can't eat 'em now. I'll have to eat 'em meself'.
Yeah?
Sorry,
getting off the track. No more brandy Mandy!

Let's put it this way:
we used to chew on stale Lyon's sliced bread
& now we wake up to cream buns.
Something in me was knowing it was just a matter of time
before someone came & breathed on them with their
oily bubble poison-breath.   Sorry.
I wouldn't mind a strong cup of *Camp*.
Five minutes? OK.

Life was sweet there.
Dad used to sing in *The Red Cow*,
doing his Sinatra act, when he wasn't collecting glasses
& making himself useful for a bit of dough.

Doing not much in fact.
I was on the building site across Sheen Road.
Big block of flats going up for peasants who
didn't live in our castle; charge hand I was, right?
Ned assistant to the caretaker of a private school
on Richmond Hill; & Eunice doing her bit in a nursery
on the hill, cooking & shopping too, obviously.

Walks along the river, couple of pints
in one of their top-notch boozers, pick-
nicks in Richmond Park watching the deer.
One bloody enormous cream bun mate —
then with a big black fly stuck in the cream
and going to the toilet in it. Right?
So, Ioanna.

To understand how she came to come along
you've got to understand dad a bit.
I don't mean understand.
I mean see what's in front of your peepers.
Dad's got something. Don't ask me what it is.
I don't know.
I don't WANT to know.
But whatever it is it means he can draw
the ladies …
Old ones, young ones, borrowed ones,
blue ones, some as big as your head (*laughs*).
The singing helps; but it's not just that.

So, this Ioanna Panagiotidou ran an after-
hours club in an alleyway off the Green, right?
A gentleman's club for blokes who are not.
She would come in *The Red Cow* for a drink &
to spread the word about her 'club'.
She hooks up with dad. You can't blame him.

Because Christ, she had her points.
Flashing eyes or what!
Talk about Black-Eyed Suzie.
Egg-timer figure. Big eyes under
all that hair like a storm. Tall (seemed
she could carry dad under her arm). She walks
in the boozer & the Red Sea parts right?
& on the first night there's dad singing
Guess I'll hang my tears out to dry.
OK?

He didn't have to tell us what was going on.
Thick as they were, we could hear
through the walls.
What could we hear?
Just don't ask.
You don't want to know.
We would hear the up & down loud &
quiet of her chat, then silence
Then … you just don't want to know.

At the time it seemed strange; but later
it did not seem strange AT ALL.
Her plan grew clear.
I mean that she would wash his clothes in the sink.
Then hang them around the place to dry.

You walked into his billet & it looked like
The Hall of the Mountain King or whatever it is,
a cave of grey tapestries, stalactites dripping
from the doors, door knobs, dining chairs, even the sink.
& one time his long johns caught fire
before the electric fire. Smoke & stink or what!
It was funny but how could we laugh?

Then Miss Panagiotidou gets a sudden fit of
gen-er-os-ity.
Usually dad paid for everything.
But she brings him this huge wooden clothes horse.
Not the usual kind, but really tall, tapers to the top
with a top rail to hang long garments, like a steeple,
folding steeple, in two halves.
Imagine like when you make a tent of a book.
And at the wide bottom, grids for laying out wet woollens.
& very thick wooden feet like boots.

"This is daft dad," we told him.
"Throw a sheet over & boy scouts can camp
in it," we joked him.
& as I was looking at it I spotted little flies
around the base of it, then all over the billet they were.
Was there a nest? No nest.
But the base was spotted.
Lots of little black spots, like blackheads on a nose.
Wood a bit soft too.

Woodworm.
"Don't be soft," says dad. "Who looks a gift horse
in the mouth." He thought he was being clever & *he*
was being soft.
"I'll put it to Io," said the soft bugger.
I was there when he "put it to Io."

She says more or less this:

"Eets very fine. Eets veentage piece Lays-eh.
Cost me week waygees.
Hay, tell you what …
I get my cheepee friend Simon to inject-eh
some lotion to eet to keel all woodworms
that is nowt there — ha ha ha — aiyneeway.
Good as gold hees wood treatyment.
Horse be bayterr then ever. No?"

So she gets this 'Simon Jenkins' chappy — sometimes
she says he's a carpenter, sometimes an upholsterer,
sometimes a 'wood scienteest' — to come along. The idea
is that he'll inspect the wormy horse, give his scientific views,
& treat it with some stuff.   Funny

        little fellow, very low centre of gravity, like a lot
of older Greek blokes it did occur to me. Would pass
for a Greek. So who can you trust, eh?
Nobody, as it turns out.   & come to think
of it: if Greek geezers have such low centres of gravity
why aren't Greeks better at football? (*laughs*)

No trace of a foreign accent but he gave off a whiff
of the Mediterranean, if you know what I mean.
"No sweat fellow," he says, "this here is clear water.
These flies ain't the woodworm flies. They's flies of the kind
that *colonise* the abandoned labyrinths of the woodworm proper.
They do not bother to burrow & they do not like to eat wood
any more than we do.
They are clear water my friend."

So what are they called? I ask him.

"Oh … they're called Tetzi … I mean Tetsickle flies.
Look 'em up. Very harmless indeed.
Soon go away. No sweat."

So why are you treating the wood? I say.
"Oh," he says, "just to help them in their battle against
the few remaining woodworm-proper who may have been
left behind."

        So, he gets out this can — like an oil can —
        which is sort of appropriate (*laughs*) but with
a narrower spout & he squirts this stuff in the holes
for a couple of minutes singing to himself.

"Job done,' he says. That'll be 14/6 ha'penny. Wish I could
make it less dough but it's the bloody blinking credit squeeze.
You won't be troubled no more my friend. This is sweet."

He left & left a smell like meths. It was meths, as it
turns out …   Now at this point I have
to introduce another character. He is a fellow inmate
of the Alms Houses. His name is Colin deFreville (real name
Keith West). An *actor*. He's got one of these faces
you would half-recognise from telly plays or B-feature
films, playing small parts: snooty shop-assistant, the bent
solicitor of a pimp, school-master bullied by his pupils.
    Very straight back, always a scarf, long coat, cane,
gestures at if you are ten yards away.
    You know the type.
It's relevant that he lived right upstairs from us.

Now if ever you want a quiet drink in an East Richmond
Boozer — *The Red Cow, The White Horse, The Mitre*, say —
you will know if he is there so you'll know when not to go in.
Listen outside before you enter.
If he is there, he'll be standing at the bar pretending to talk
to just one person
but really he'll be addressing the whole pub
in his stage voice AT FULL VOLUME.

"If you go to heaven," he might say, "and see a man
leaning on a five-bar gate listening for the crack
of leather on willow, then … you have found
an Englishman."
Got the idea?
    Or he will be advising Harold Macmillan,
or most likely re-telling some theatre anecdote
for the umpteenth time.
That's why we all called him *Loud Colin*.
He even called himself that. The blower goes
& it's HELLO! LOUD COLIN HERE.

So, as I say, he lived upstairs from us. Nice geezer actually.
When he wasn't being Loud Colin he would whisper
& avoid your eye, shy like. But my God could he drink,
though only drank as Loud Colin, on stage so to speak.

Loud Colin always slept late & he would slop
around the Alms Houses' quad in a dressing gown
or a thing that looked like one. Kind of garment
actors put on when they come off stage I suppose; though
he would dap over the road to the corner shop in it:
thick velvet or maybe chenille, high collar or hood,
dragon type image on the back, tied up
with a long cord like a curtain pull.
Maybe he wore his jim-jams under it …
we found out he did indeed wear them in,
as they say, 'tragic circumstances.'

We had told Loud Colin about the wormy horse
& that Ioanna was sending someone called Simon
round to sort it out that morning.
That morning he was up in his billet doing what
he called 'taking coffee' & looking out of the window
at Simon leaving & saying over his shoulder
"all sorted maties."

Colin shouts & you would have been able
to hear him in Twickenham:
"STOP YOU … " the word he used I would not quote
in mixed company.
"HE'S ONE OF HER BUBBLES. A GREASEBALL.
HE'S NOT SIMON: HE'S CHRISTO GEORGIOU
FROM BRENTFORD"

He's incensed, & no mistake; & now tragedy
takes the wheel.

He dashes out of his billet down the narrow
stone stairs at a pace to get down to chase this not-

Simon.   Now you have to understand
that the cord of his dressing gown was very long &
that it snakes down around his feet at this time
like two anacondas with a will of their own
dancing their heads around his stockinged feet.
It seems that one of them got wrapped round his knee
just as he trod on the other & goes
arse over tit (pardon my French)
down the stone steps, landing at our feet like the cord
had lassoed a bag of bones of its very own purpose.

Upshot is: ambulance to St George's Hospital,
traction, concussion, operation on his back.
Upshot is: Loud Colin is more or less dead,
though a whispering Keith lives on.
        Now here's a theme to return to people:
Christo's uncle gets Loud Colin's billet.
So neat it makes you sick.

                                        & talking of neat,
this brings me neatly back to dad
putting his foot through the floor.
        After Loud Colin's accident we as a family
were all bound up with it — going to see
what was left of him & all the rest of it. So, we ignored
the fact that the wooden horse was still in dad's billet
& we pretend to ourselves that there are fewer little flies
while all the time the parasites were invading
fresh territory —
their secret industry — while dad slept, though less
often with the Greek bint, it has to be said.

So, he gets up one morning & puts his foot
through the floorboards on his way to the bog.
They were the original boards,
used to be oak so hard you'll think you could
get a spark out of it & now it's like
the inside of a *Crunchy Bar* or an *Aero Bar*

or a blend of the two.
Dad goes ballistic & chucks the clothes horse
out the door & into the quad. The Alms House authorities
get alarmed, then suspicious. Of course, somebody calls round.
First the chappy who was no more than a caretaker
really. "Sorry Les mate. Gotta report this." Then dad gets
a letter warning of an 'official visitation'. I made sure
I was there to keep an eye on him.

Two people. A speechless bint
with a clip-board who looked
like she worked in a prison run by nuns
& an ex-army geezer — hair cut into the wood, staccato,
little 'tosh, trouser creases you could cut cheese with.
Refused the offer of tea; threatening toe-caps.
Cut a long story short, they decide to
'investigate' him — meaning to check all the documents
that prove he *bona fide* deserves to be there so we
bona fide deserve to be there to support him.
Nothing wrong with these documents mind
(*takes*
a break to laugh to himself & blow his nose). I paid
good money for them from the geezer in
the Mortlake boozer.

I've got to explain now. There are a number of ways
you can be eligible to be in the Alms Houses.
One of them is to be 'an impoverished ex-combatant
of Her Majesty's Armed Forces, especially gentlemen
who acquired physical of mental disabilities
during the period of combat'.
Dad was supposed to have served
in the First World War in the trenches where
he 'acquired' shell shock. That's what
the forged record said anyway. & boy did he play
up to this. If he saw
one of the 'custodians' or one of the Alms House
Committee in the quad he'd go into his act —

throw one arm over his head & glide sideways as
he says "Ring the bell for Mary's lost in corn.
Tie acorns to Tony Prince." & if he met an inmate
who he didn't trust he'd shout random bits of German.
                    Given his delicate situation
he needed people he could trust (his son) to give
him 'emotional succour'. So, I support him through
the wall as he supports Ioanna or some other
lucky bint.   Lucky sod he is:
just too young for the first war and just too old for
the second. As for 'support' you see dad
& see a super-healthy ferret who's game for a laugh.

We wait three weeks for the outcome of the investigation.
Amazed that all is fine & they apologise.
Dad goes across the road to *The Red Cow* to celebrate.
Sees Ioanna there, causes a scene, accuses her at
Loud Colin volume of deliberately infecting the wood
of his billet through the clothes horse.   People
in the bar make no sense of it, the stew of phrases —
clothes horse, Simon Bloody Georgiou, poor poor Colin,
Crunchy Bar
"want to get us out & your bubbles in."

She stands proud & takes it with a smile, calls round
the next day in manner of a district nurse.
I happened to be there. & she's …

"OK leetle bowlocks-for-brayns-eh.
You have cost me custom een my club-eh,
you dameege-eh my repeetation as a
BEEZINESS woman, een the eyes of the
peoples. You pay-eh the price-eh.
I write an anowneejmaus letter-eh
to the custoees & the Alms comtee. I tell all
about the pay to the geezer-eh een
the Mortlake-eh pub.
Be cheerybye-eh to you deeks. Owkay-eh?"

& that's exactly what she did.
We thought it was bluster; but two weeks later
the ex-army geezer comes with a posh geezer.
No warning — just turns up early in the morning.
They took our precious documents away & the posh one
turns as he leaves & says do we have a lawyer? No mate.
Prepare for the worst, he goes.
We didn't & then the worse turns up, right?

Would have been less bad if they had just
chucked us out — possessions on the quad grass, sort of idea:
blankets, knives forks & spoons, hot water bottles.
Cheerio then.
Instead, they first withdraw our privileges —
no night key, so we all have to be in by nine.
Can't go in the TV room & the pool room.
We have to estimate our weekly spending & reveal
what they call our 'assets'. They can come
into our billets by the master key whenever
they like. Worse of all, the other inmates know
all about it; some stick by us — some, a few,
one or two.

We had a month to get out.
Where to?

Now this is the killer …
They would keep turning up with what they called
'candidates for Alms support' to view our billets
& OK you will have guessed:
many many bubbles come. They would come
with the ex-army geezer who would stand erect & quiet
while they lift our family photos to look & snigger,
open cupboards & sniff, bounce on the bed & say
"Them spreeengs ain't up-a to much.
Chuck da bloody bloody thing away-eh,"
spend 10 minutes in the bog; tell us to give them
a fag, talk in their own lingo & ignore us.

We were being invaded by a killing army,
punished.
OK, we deserved to be punished.
We lied & deprived
worthy old warriors of two sweet billets.
Well charge us with a crime, OK?
I did the fraud. Put me in clink,
but leave my family a drop of dignity.
Let's be fair.

They came in — the cheeky bubbles & the
short-back-&-sides merchants & took our home
away. Yeah, we stole something
from some old warrior or some skint geezer
contemplating the rest-of-his-life as a tramp, beggar,
or housebreaker.
But we did not steal
A HOME HE ALREADY HAD.
        No such thing as a future home, future
billet yes, no such thing as a home-to-come any more
than a past-to-come.
A home is part of you & who you have been, where
you have come from; it's imprints of the parts
of a world that mean things to you.
If you cannot see this, then all I can say is

Heavens to Betsy. (*He pauses, grins, puts his head
in his hands briefly, then goes on.*)

& I would get visits from other inmates saying:
"Scuse us!" and barge past me into the living room.
"Just wanna little look around." They had applied to
change billets, had their eye on a ground floor place
& were sizing it up. "I think I'll stick my radiogram
there" kind of thing.

I can't honestly say this made me happy.
But one day there was a turn up.
I get a visit & I thought — another bloody bubble.
But no. Geezer standing there
in three-piece suit, stiff collar, watch chain,
all polished & old, an old-style gent, a buffer ...
a proper buffer.
"May I come in," he says, "I have some communications
that may interest you." Turns out he's just taken the bus
down from Kew Green. Posh, but in a correct
kind of way.   His knees
creaked when he sat down to have the tea I made him.
Turns out he has a niece who is one of my mother's nurses;
so, he hears about me & because he's local he heard
about my trouble.   Thing is you see I kept all this quiet
from mum on account of our naughtiness with the documents.
Mum's very upstanding — in some ways; some of the time.

Very nice geezer, very grateful for the arrowroot
biscuits. But, sounds strange to say it:
he seemed sort of two-dimensional; if could have nipped
round to the side of him
fast as light he'd be as thin as paper.   Plus,
he had one of mum's mannerisms: when he ended an
important sentence, especially with a bad message to it,
he would drop his jaw like he was shocked by what
he'd found himself saying.
Tell you what — what I heard both shocked me for the fact
but not for the novelty; if you get my drift.

"You ever wonder why it's mainly Greek gentlemen & ladies
who have been filling these desirable niches or short-listed
to fill them?" he goes.
I said I was too wrapped up in the bloody horror to wonder.

This is it.   Of course
it was all about Ioanna — the creature who is both
a seducing woman who'll weasel into your life to make it
wormy rotten at the core, & is like a powerful spirit above
it all too alien to grasp.
This 'gentleman's club' of hers. As we kind of knew,
it was more or less a knocking shop; & that's less
than half of it: the girls are mainly from the local schools
and under age, well under, it turns out.
With the bigger picture being that her clubs are all over the place,
as far east as Brixton, Clerkenwell, Camberwell & each one caters
for particular tastes: blokes who like blokes, blokes who like blokes
to beat them up, blokes who like bints to beat them up
or walk on them in heels, bints who like bints & quite a few
for blokes who like bints so young they're hardly bints at all.

"It beggars belief," & his jaw drops. The next bit is very easy
to believe:
"A not inconsiderable number of the custodians of this establishment
are patrons on the club off Richmond Green. Miss Panagiotidou
is of the view that unless these fellows give special preference
to her fellow nationals, she feels she should tell their wives
or mothers, their employers or peers." Big jaw drop.
                    Well, he tells me the custodians say 'alright dear,
once they fall empty we will, but we can't just throw the geezers out.
Questions will be asked. Maybe you can help us make them
fall empty' … 'Oh, I can do that', says Miss Pana-got-to-go-too.
Dad was easy meat of course
& the wooden clothes horse was her enjoying her work.

So, he told me these facts & with me well told
he shifted gear from upright buffer to weirdly
jolly uncle & popped off smartly, patting me
on the arm saying: "Good luck with this
Sonny Jim."

You can imagine that where he had jaw-drops I had
teeth-grinds. I wanted to kill Ioanna.
Armed with these facts I could kill her business
& smile to myself as she finds herself banged up in Holloway.
See if she can get a laugh out of that! I'd tell the coppers
or maybe sell my story to *The Daily Mirror*.
        But the thought of doing it
made me feel dirty & scared. Dirty because it's
being a tell-tat-tit, a nark; scared … well,
you cut off the head of one of the snaky necks of the bubble mafia
and nine more bite you in the arse — pardon my French.

Now I have to own up that when I'm in a quandary like this
I phone my mother, who some of you will know as
Baroness Clifton of Haselmere. I kid you not.
Could hardly get across the road to the call box
for all the half-crowns in my pocket. Knew it would be
a long call.   This was her, give or take.

"Dahrling, precious, don't do it. Don't act. This is not
the way things should turn out at all. It's not
just creepy & dangerous: it goes against
you & your plotted future dahrling.

        This huge anger flaring up is two bad
things welded together into a contradictory badness:
it's not you, a loving almost pious man; & it's *too much*
of you. I mean it's self-centred, an indulgence, dahrling:
an itch you are determined to scratch knowing it will
come back ten times worse after the first bliss of scratching.
        Do your duty by your father, son … & wife. I know
the old ram seems indestructible but his winning streak is only that;
I know your son is something of a Big Soft Nelly but he is your son
& has plenty of room for growth, like well-bought school shoes; yes,
and Eunice is a *terribly* useful little person to have around.

Prepare for your departure from these Alms-nonsenses.
To my mind they were only ever a holiday let, not a home —
despite your rhapsodising ruminations on what is & is not
a home."

The last bit is rubbish but I took her advice.
I bit my tongue about the facts from the buffer & prepared
for the following Tuesday, the day by which we had to leave.
All I did to prepare was to call a bloke called Ern Bacon.
Used to work for him in removals. Bacon's Better Removals.
He had one huge van & he owed me a favour & two weeks' wages.
Not a bad geezer at all; just prone to running out of dough.

"Yeah," says Ern, "I can move you & your stuff. Tell you what:
I know of a place going for a cheap rent up in Turnham Green.
Not too bad."

The day arrived. A very windy day. Our stuff was blown all over
the quad & out to Sheen Road. Dark too, like tea-time in January;
though it was a spring morning. Ern was blocking the traffic
in Sheen Road, cars
having to queue to get past him.
We're ferrying stuff out, weaving under the weight, cussing.
Anyway, I'd found quite a clean sack & put lots of Eunice's
pots & pans in it, the po, my spanners, nothing big & told
Eunice she could carry it out while the men carried the breakables.
Assumed she was behind me as I reminded her she had a shift
at *The White Horse* that night, so get the dinner on boiling early.

Looked round & all I could see was the sack.
I saw the Tooting bus stuck behind Ern,
heard Ern say he's seen the wife jump on.
I dashed onto the bus. No sign at all.
"Probably hiding under a seat," laughs old Ern.
Very funny. You don't know the power
of Ioanna, was what I thought to myself.

Three: Wanderings

So, we were three not-happy cheated cheaters
in Ern's wagon. I was thinking about Eunice; Ned was thinking,
probably, about his mother; dad was thinking, probably, about how
he could light a fag while standing up and holding on to the side-rails
that secured the furniture to the wagon. Yes, all standing
as if waiting for somebody to turn up. Would Eunice ever?
Doubtful. She was probably then slaving over a moussaka
in a basement kitchen watched by a bubble matron
dressed all in black.

We *were*
standing up till Ern took a left turn at East Sheen
up the South Circular & we all fell over —
THWACK!!!
Who would try to stand up again? Ned would;
& he crashed over when Ern took a right & all
our stuff slid over the floor. For some seconds
I wondered if Ern might be an agent of Ioanna & we
were being captured. In the end we treated it like
one of those fairground attractions. Pay good
money for this, some folks would.

Turnham Green. Yeah, sweet. The touch of Richmond
surprised me as I think of moving east as moving to
Hammersmith or Shepherd's Bush.
Basement flat. Very dark, made the weather look sunny.
One bedroom, little kitchen, teeny living room.
"Cosy," Ned goes. "This'll do," says dad.
                    I went to speak, but sneezed,
went to speak again & sneezed again (funny, when I'm tired
I think the past tense of 'sneeze' is 'snoze'). This told me
cats had lived here. Cats bring the plague to me,
so I had to leave, telling Ned what to do about cleaning

& thinking what a good investment that second-hand *Goblin*
was — get those hairs sucked up. Bleach & plenty of it;
rosewater, essence of any citrus fruit, make a wood fire, sprinkle
all surfaces with water, open all windows (none would open).

Bought some spuds, packet of *Trex*, tin of corned beef. Corned beef
& chips: thought we'd have that for tea.
That settled us; then off to the nearest boozer
& four pints for me.
Slept like a log, but God what a dream:
I was coming back to this flat in a blizzard,
walking down the iron steps to the basement I saw a light
all pink & welcoming — spam pink plus the sound of frying.
On the door was a brass knocker in the shape of
a man's head. Round face, long locks of hair like sunbeams.
I lifted it to knock for entry & the face scrunches up in anger
to say: "Ow! Be careful! Wrap on the door with your knuckles
till they bleed. Have a care, you brazen lump."
I recognised the face & voice — old Potter,
my geography teacher from schooldays
— silly little sod but we were petrified of him.
"Listen Hale," he says, "you live in a fool's paradise.
You know you can't stay here. I know the lay of this land.
& I know this Turnham island of pleasantness
with its green & genteel folk in pubs with hanging baskets
is alien to you. Alien to what fate has in store for you.
This is not your proper home.
You must make your own home
out of your thin materials & ambiguous offspring.
Heed the words of an unquiet spirit. I'm neither above
nor below & not of the earth any more.
I'm a fixture or minor element. Next week I may be
a light-switch, dado rail, newel: by which I mean
if you touch me it will be the worse for you young
fellow-me-lad.
I've heard you say things like 'I can't see for looking.'
Stop your wet effort & be a man — but elsewhere."

This made me angry: dream angry like you are drunk
in charge of yourself. I grabbed the knocker &
he bit me, blood flowed from my finger that looked black
in the blizzard light. No pain, just an itch. This made
the anger worse. I yanked the knocker from the
door. Potter squealed & black blood pumped like battle
vomit from the hole. It was the source of all black blood.

I woke sweating & must have shouted out:
"Told you not to finish those pickled eggs," said dad
& went back to sleep.

The next few days & many many days after were filled
with dad & Ned going on about how good it was round there.
Dad had found a pub to sing in & a job selling boot polish
& brushes door to door; Ned had three paper-rounds,
mornings & tea-times, & a job handing out towels
in a posh baths in Chiswick; I worked in *The Home & Colonial.*
They thought they were all set up & dandy.
I thought I should consult the oracle.

[*He then launches into a long account*
of how one can use the Chinese Book on Divination or I Ching
to predict the future by throwing three coins six times
to build hexagrams.
It takes a while for him to realise he has lost the audience &
finally suggests a bar break. Some leave; but the poshos are all in situ.]

So, I ask the oracle: "What's my future in Turnham Green?"
& they say — I say 'they' because I think of it as they —
say Standstill leading to Wounded Light. Wounded Light!
I ask what is the consequence of putting down roots here
& the answer is Exhausting Restriction; no second hexagram —
just that. Changing to nothing, never changing.

Pure & simple & bad enough for me to believe it.
Then I ask the consequence of moving north, south, east
& west. For the first three nothing really, could mean or half-

mean things tepid & dull, not even a bit of honest ambiguity,
just a cloud hiding another cloud; but for west it said
Peace leading to a funny one that means among other things
Founding a Dynasty. Can't say fairer than that.   Yes,
I do say things like: 'Can't see for looking' &, yes, I know
it's a wet thing to say; but when it's something true
& clear you want & that's all you want, you should not *look*
for it: it will show itself to you. Thank goodness
for the *Ching*, I say.

I go to the call box & ask Ern if he knows about
a billet going West of here.
"Feeling ready for a challenge?" he goes.
I think a bit at this & then he says:
"You'll pay less for a whole half of a house,
bogs upstairs, little bit of garden, quiet area,
in West Ealing. Right near a park like lots of Ealing is.
I'll have to charge you for the move this time."
"OK," I say.

Back at the flat I keep pointing out how cramped it is,
pretending to trip over things and fall into walls, trying
to bring them round to the idea of moving
to a bigger billet. How wonderful that would be.
They don't agree, so I just tell them we're moving
& Bob's your uncle we moved.

When the moving day came we all had different ideas
about how to deal with the journey. I decide to sit
in a fireside chair with my feet hooked around
a side rail, but keeping ready to move side-on and grab the rail;
Ned decided that sitting on the floor of the wagon
would not be so bad if he could strap a cushion
to his backside to stop those vibrations shuddering
up his body; Dad decided to sit or kneel on a suitcase
containing all the breakables he cared about
(framed photos of ex-bints, whiskey tumblers,
champagne glasses with memories attached)
said he'd ride it like a horse.

Made no odds. We all ended up being sloshed to one side
or the other & being thrown forward
when Ern braked. He charged us for broken crockery being over the van
& bent side-rails.

We arrive there.

When we get out it's like we've not really arrived
anywhere at all. Or we could be anywhere in England's
suburbia, anywhere. Never felt farther from the river.
Actually, it was … OK.
What made it not completely boring was the clever idea
somebody had had to black out one of the houses
in the row, like actors black out teeth. Maybe
      it was done as part of some street party.
You could get the local kids to chalk on the walls
like a blackboard for a laugh. Dad's sight is bad so
the blacking out trick worked on him.
"What a tiny bombsite," he goes. "Very neat too."

"There she is," Ern goes. "Your new rental.
You've heard of The Pink Un. This is The Black Un.
You're 29A not 29." & he clears off.

All the brickwork was painted with a kind of black distemper
& the woodwork was a mid-grey. Two front doors right next
to each other.   Inside
it was OK. No need to share rooms for sleeping.
No sounds from next door.
      Pub nearby called The Plough. Sort of estate pub.
We just dumped our stuff inside & wandered down there.
Came back merry in a resigned lost way with steak & kidney pies
we'd eat cold, & a bunch of bananas.

As we got back the geezer from number 31 was putting
his key in the lock. Indian geezer.

"You met Mrs Harpic yet?" he says, friendly.

"No."

"You will matey. You'll know when you have."

"Who is she?" I ask.

"Your very next-door neighbour, number 29."

"Why do you call her Mrs Harpic?"

"Well, her old man is an Austrian refugee. Jewish chap
I think, works nights, little bald chap. We hardly ever see him.
She always talks about him as 'Herr Pick'. You know
'Herr Pick likes his liver & onions'. Don't know his first
name … Heinz, Heinrich, Adolf … ha-ha. Oh dear oh dear.
She's a bit of a toff in her way & her 'Herr Pick' sounds like
Harpic. Plus … how to put this? … that the word makes you think
of toilets is spot on. You'll see
what I mean. We *all* call her Mrs Harpic.
Good luck chaps."

Next morning

I'm mooching about the little back garden & I hear
a rasping voice like a crow or crone say:

"Keeping well?"

Over the rickety wooden fence I see a face,
not the face of some old bird but the face
of a girl, with piercing eyes & a smile
that was taking the Mickey. I told her how
we came to be there
while she kept yawning.
I moved closer & saw over the fence that she was not
standing but squatting on a water butt,
her knees up by her chin; wearing black leggings
and a multi-coloured mohair pullover

that looked like feathers.
She was heavily pregnant.
I assumed she was anyway.
She seemed both too young and too old
to be up the spout.
The small talk was very small indeed & she soon said
"I'll pop in to see you later with some magazines for you
to read in Blondin Park … Got to go now.
Must tune in to *Lift up Your Hearts* on the wireless
& have my morning cocoa."

She gets down from the barrel and — don't really
know how to put this — but she loudly blew off
no 'blew' sounds wrong, blowed off, no that's worse;
oh, she loudly farted — sorry —
like a little clap of thunder.
& worse luck the wind was in the wrong direction.
She scoots indoors with amazing speed like
a feathery balloon blown by the wind. In fact, I
could swear that she was blown in by her own wind,
sounded like a two-stroke: a *BSA Bantam*, say.

I couldn't think of her just then, not so close after
the event; and anyway, she was beyond thinking about.
So, I went up the road to look at this Blondin Park,
named after Charles Blondin, the geezer who walked across
Niagara Falls on a tightrope & lived around here. Why?
So, what could a park be like
that inspired a feathery fart machine like her to give
us magazines to read in? I imagined

a perfect English Park, the sort you see drawn
in kids' books: boating lake, gaily-painted bandstand, playground
with all the rides & things, deckchairs for magazine reading,
kids flying kites with their dads, benches for old folks
to watch the kiddies sailing their boats.
Nothing, no more

than a flat grassed area before allotments,
some tarmac paths, some scrubby trees round a football pitch.
A perfect park? Oh yes, perfect for this area.

I walked on the grass — tufty, too tufty
for kids to play football, let alone cricket.
Imagined the three of us lying on the tufty grass
with our magazines reading out bits to one another.

Dad & Ned had been up to the Broadway all day
looking for work — shops, building sites, you know.
I had been shopping & bought food you didn't need
to cook for our tea: a nice white tin loaf, cheese,
sausage rolls, jam doughnuts. We were just starting
in on it, when the knocker goes.

"Here I am!" & she pushes past me & in
carrying a pile of magazines. That we were
having our tea — she ignores it; & hands out our magazines.
For Ned:
four copes of *Spic & Span* & four copies of *Heath*
& Efficiency.
You probably know folks that these pretend to be
about keeping fit & Nature but really the point of them
is to show photos of naked bints with their — what
shall I say — bints' *areas* covered in something
like putty.

"Read these in your bedroom is my advice to you,"
she goes. As she was doing this

I noticed her hands. Much bigger than you would expect
& her finger-nails were incredibly long & pointed
& painted bright red, like she had just scratched
somebody to death. It went through me to look at them.

For dad, she had lots of *Readers' Digests*. Fine,
but they were sort of rusty, covered in what I hoped
were stains of brown rust & with the pages sticking together.
For me, there were some very old copies of *Titbits*. They had
lots of photos cut out so when you turned a page it came away
in little bits.

"Thanks very much," I said, my mind not really on the mags
but on two of her habits, that maybe she kept for indoors.
She was forever picking her nose & it looked like the pickings
stayed behind on her killer nails.   She was also fond —
how shall I put this? Let's just say fond of scratching her arse.

Of course, dad noticed this & of course dad is less polite
than me so he goes:

"Got a bit of meat in your tooth darling?"

She didn't reply to this but did all of a sudden show
an interest in our tea. She picked up the loaf —
"Where on earth did you buy this, fellows?"
She fingered the cheese —
"This should be under cover. Let it sweat a bit."
She prodded the sausage rolls & the doughnuts.
When some fell on the floor she bent down to pick them up
& let out a fart: not of the thunderclap kind but one
that was very low, steady, strong, & long. Also,
if somebody with perfect pitch had heard it, like
our Brian, he could tell you the note. C-sharp, say.

"I always say to myself," she said to us, "wherever you be
let the wind be free." Then she laughed so much she made
herself sneeze & did not make herself clean up the result
of the sneeze from her belly-top or the table cloth.
        She was about to leave but caught sight of
my copy of the *I Ching*, saying:

"Tell me. From which arse did this explode?"

"It's mine."

"I'll see you tomorrow Eddy old son."

We couldn't bear to touch the food, though we were
all starving. Went out to look for a chip shop.
"Well, she seems very nice," said dad.

They did find work but the next day I stayed
home to … potter about. Was sitting down to
Workers' Playtime with a cup of tea when
the knocker goes & in she comes carrying
some thick old-looking books.

"Don't bother with that Chinky rubbish. I'll show you
how it's done. You want to know your future? What
do you want to know Eddy Boy?"
Well, I have to admit, I'm always interested in the future.
I mean, when I'm in the present, not when
it becomes the present & then it loses its interest.
— ha-ha.
Though, to be honest with you,
I have a weak-minded side too, so I just told her.

"I want to know whether it's a good idea to leave London
& go to the West Country — "

"Sit!"

She got out a pack of funny-looking cards, put it to one side, asked
my date & time of birth, wrote it down & grabbed my hands
one by one. It was painful, this. Those bloody nails,
like sharpened razor clams.
First the left ("What you begin with")
Then the right ("What you have done with it

& what is in store").

Then she got me to play a kind of patience,
— plus 20 questions with the cards —
all the while sniggering & chanting
"The Book of Froth is the Book of Life."
Then she opened four of the big old books & looked up
thing after thing; which took a long time.

Now, I know this is a bit disgusting. It is. It was.
But while she was doing this she must have been
releasing a string of silent-but-deadlies.
I had go out to the garden to escape the pong. Eventually,
she hammers on the window & squawks for me to come back
so she can give her verdict on it all. Now, I could swear
her belly has gone down a good few inches since she arrived.

"I suppose the good news is that you will establish
a kind of home in the West.   But
it's a thin-walled home whose walls leak everything into the world.
& let in all the wrong kinds of air.
Walls like clear glass — so it will feel as if you lived
in a field, not in a house. Before you even manage this
you will have to endure unimaginable hunger that will cause
you to eat cardboard to fill your empty bellies.
That is not the worst of it.

There will be impassable opposition to you
from people who think you have stolen *their* home.
Blood upon blood will be spilt from gouging & slashing —
razor-sharp blades flashing in the sun …
Oh, got any biscuits? … Good, stay here.
I'll get them."

She dashed into the kitchen & found our packet
of *Rich Tea*, slashed it open with her nails along the length
& went through them like it was one of those card indexes,
picked out two then cleared off suddenly.
I threw the rest away — stands to reason.

It was an unspoken thing between us that we couldn't
stay there long.
Meanwhile, I had to get a job to help with the rent.
I worked behind the bar in *The Plough*.
        Sounds like one bad thing after another this;
well, now things get a bit better — for a bit.

We'd just opened for the evening trade & I was
polishing glasses. Place nearly empty & this tall brunette
wanders in. I sort of recognised her without actually
knowing who she was. She orders a Bloody Mary.
"Ed, if I'm not mistaken," she goes.
Turns out she is Ann-Marie from The Alms Houses.
She'd been married to Harold Spector, a bit of a mate
of mine. I didn't know him there, but he had, like me,
been at Monte Casino; wasn't as lucky as me —
or braver. Who knows? Braver.
Very badly injured; but not a broken man.
Hero in a manner of speaking.
Ann-Marie had stuck by him despite her, well,
liking a lively life, let's say.   So, of course,
Harold & her had been there all legit.
        He'd died a couple of years ago.
I'd heard stories about her after she'd left (had to,
like us).
Shacked up with old Harry Webb of Webb Bros Builders —
a very big geezer in West London, I can tell you.
See, she seems — I say seems, leave it at that —
to go for blokes with power; like Harold Spector was
& old Webby is; & they treat her a bit like
a trophy. After all, she is a prize: a very smart
bit of crackling; smart-clever, smart & well-
turned-out; and, you know, smart *as a bint is*.
                    So, it turns out
she's now married again & living In Chiswick.
Had just popped up here to see her solicitor
up on the Green; had come in for what she called
'a snifter' after the meeting.

We chatted about this and that; she listened
to our sad story about the f … about the bubbles;
& she is sympathetic while still flashing smiles
& says:
"Oh, you must come to dinner, just you.
Meet Julius. He's a psychiatrist in private practice.
Get the bus to Kew Bridge, walk along Strand
on the Green by the river towards Chiswick;
we're off that. Here's the address."
All brisk. Mind you, she always was. Never took
to the Alms Houses, if I recall.
We arranged a day, and I went there.

Never seen anything like it.
No front room. A big room with
a kitchen at one end, easy chairs, bloody *cello*
in the corner on a stand.
No wallpaper & no painted wood
to speak of. Bare wood.
All these white walls' abstract pictures
on the walls, nice nick-knacks here & there.
& he was doing the cooking — the hubby.
Spaghetti Bolognaise, & red wine to drink;
bit of modern jazz playing in the background.
No telly on.

"I hope you like this plonk," he goes
all posh & smooth, deep voice like an announcer.
Looks like he's got to shave twice a day. Short hair; black.
Black thick horn-rims. Serious glasses, though he made little funnies.
        After the nosh — very nice — Ann-Marie does the
washing up while Jules (he said to call him) & I have brandy
& one of those little cigars each.

"Something is troubling you both at a deep & at a shallow level,"
he goes.

"Yes," I go.

"The deep level is easy to see: you need a home, a secure base
from which you can explore a new world. You demand both
novelty and the well-known: exciting bracing novelty;
& the warm familiar."

"Yes," I go.

"Well, that's not so unusual. You say you know where you want
to go: to the West Country. In passing I — I mean we —
have a holiday home in my beloved Cornwall. Mevagissey. Do you know it
at all? No. But there is a mental brake on this desire. You are being
held back from bringing it to fruition. Now I think I can persuade you
that this is indeed a shallow concern and that you can dissolve it."

"Could be Jules," I go. Then I told him about Mrs Harpic &
her prediction.

"Ah ha!" he laughs, "Harpics are everywhere. Farting necromancers,
clawed diviners fill the groaning shelves of our mental libraries.
You have a mind too open to suggestion springing from fantasy, a good
mind but one to which ordure easy adheres. Please listen to what
I have to say. Two pieces of advice: one will be about what
you have to avoid or rather steer between; and two about how
to seek advice from one who can indeed make a fair fist
at prediction. One based on facts of past history & the science
of depth psychology; rather than on the deliverances
of the bogie-encrusted pages of sidereal tables. Top up?"

"Yes please," I go.

"You have to find a clear path Ed between two dangers.
On the one hand, you must avoid capture by strong emotions.
You think an emotion like resentment, distrust,
some hot sneaking superstition is something you can just dip
your toe into, as it were; indeed, something whose force
will carry you *forward*.
In your case: not so. Your emotional field

is that of a whirlpool. The force is circular, sucking
you down to a drowning eye, having swirled you round
till your sense is gone. Otherwise, you think the upward thrust —
& note how this rhymes with 'lust' — of a positive emotion
can elevate you. Oh sure it will — dangerously high & then
like a tap turned off, it drops you down to the fatal focal
of the familiar whirlpool.
        Breathe & think deeply, is my advice to you.
The other adjacent danger is more subtle & more external
than internal. You are lured by the attractions of a project
or of a person. This may not evoke any strong emotion.
You might see the positives coolly & with nuance, take
a balanced view & decide yes you will proceed. But your perception
can only be of the surface, by which I mean the project (say)
has to you only an uppermost & visible
come-hither property.
But surely this come-hither property cannot be
come-hither
all the way down?
What supports the come-hither? Just as physical beauty
is grounded in the wet-ware of knotted tissue, glistening
cramped organs, & the dark tunnels of digestion,
the uppermost beauty of an idea or plan or potential girl
may rest upon processes wolfish or fishy.
These are not, *pace* Mrs Harpic, processes you must
go through: they are the inherent underpinnings,
basements & foundations. What lurks in them?
How on earth can you tell?
You cannot tell & for all you know these delightful prospects
may front or top a cave-full of victim's bones —
if I may be metaphorical.
        Now to my second
        point. Because you cannot determine what lurks
in these wolfish basement caverns you must seek the advice
of one who has fed the facts of past revelations through
the filter of depth psychology."

He then got up & fetched me a little card
with a name & phone number on it.

"Yes! One can predict the future. One can predict
it by examining the past — your own past & that of others
in relation to the 'delightful plan'; but one must do so
via an intellect informed by depth psychology … Do you
see what I'm getting at — at all?"

By this time the wine & brandy had messed me up a bit
so I go:
"Well, Jules, to tell you the truth: I think it's just a bit
of common sense dolled up with a lot of clever talk."

He then looked at me through his big black window-glasses
with his eyes little black dots of what I think was anger.
He pauses, stands up, grabs both my hands, & yells:
"GO WEST YOUNG MAN! Do tell
Ann-Marie when you are leaving & she'll turn up with
lots of jolly gifts. Now I have to say I'm a wee bit exercised
about your missing your last bus … "

I didn't phone that number the next day: I phoned
old Ern Bacon's number. Did he know of a place
we could afford west of there? Yes he did —
in Twickenham, actually in St. Margaret's, a villagey
kind of place. I told him it would do for now.

"Can't hear you very well mate. Got a clothes peg
on your conk?" He laughs. Then he warns me that
while the billet is cheap it will take a lot of work
to make it liveable. Eventually a day was fixed for the move;
& I phoned Ann-Marie, on the number she'd given me, to tell her.
She turned up with all kinds of goodies.
I went to the door though and she ignored me:
"Where's Neddy?" she says.
All over him, she was, pats him

on the bottom not at all like you would a toddler
but gives him lots of toddlery treats to eat.
For me and dad she mainly got books —
Hidden Bath, *Bristol Suspension Bridge: A Challenge Met*,
Weymouth Walks, *A History of Cider*, as well a short-sleeved
pullover each. She kissed
us all Goodbye, especially Ned.
Can't make her out at all.

We crossed Richmond Bridge into East Twickenham &
it felt like crossing into the West Country, the outer reaches of it;
though it wasn't. Took a turn right up to St Margaret's …

What a place! Lovely little red-brick terrace & inside …
imagine the pong inside the Harpic house & double it.
Someone had left a boiled ham on a shelf months ago —
maggoty; a radiogram sat in a pool of yellow water;
the bog didn't flush, in fact the plumbing was all to cock —
pardon my French. Bare wires too. A death-trap.

Now dad & me have worked for builders often enough
so we know what's what. We went off to suppliers for
plumbing, electrical, & building stuff … nearly broke the bank.
Left Ned with a simple job to do: get some planks out of the
shed & nail down floorboards. We got back

We'd forgotten to take the key & he answered
the door with a soaking wet head, like a chewed rubber
cap on his bonce. Then he sprinted into the scullery
to put his hand back over a great bloody water-spout. He'd nailed
through a mains pipe. It was snowing plaster from the
ceiling. Then we noticed a small river coming down the stairs.

"I managed to get the bog flushing though dad," he goes.

"Flushing permanently," says dad, "O grandson-of-mine."

I strapped some plumber's putty round the pipe & dad
managed to fix the flush, while Ned mopped up.
            We needed a professional in … But who?

I went round the neighbours asking.
Net curtains twitched; people came to the door blankly
saying 'not-today-thank-you'. Thought we were tinkers.
In the end a nice geezer gave me a name —
Reg Sitar.   Sounds Indian doesn't it?
"He's very cheap," he said, "needs the work.
On his uppers right now."

Reg turned up the next day & it turns out …
He's a bloody bubble; clear as day.
Full name is Reginald Sitaridou.
But he was OK actually. Felt sorry for him.
Thin as a rake, shivering like a leaf on a windy common.
You could tell he knew his stuff & he charged peanuts.
When he'd finished he told his story.
He was a gambler …

            In a boozer called *The Twisted Wheel*, down
near the river, he'd joined a card school run by
a fellow by the name of Matt Polly.
They met in the Snug, all hush-hush of course.
                        Gradually over two months, well,
he lost all his dough.   Now he can barely
afford to eat.   I tell you it completely changed
my view of our bubble friends … not of Ioanna of course.
He was human.   Ned made him loads
of cheese-on-toast, now we had the cooker working.

Ned's got a kind heart. In fact the next, actually the last,
bit is about Ned so I need to tell you about him.
You meet him & you think 'soft & dim, soft & dim',
you'll think there goes a 9-year-old in a man's body.
But put him in front of a chessboard, play a game

of cards with him, give him one of these brain teasers
you see in the papers — not a general knowledge one: one
with symbols, squiggles, not words ...
& he'll knock your socks off.

Beneath it all — & you have seen the 'it all' — is a strong brain
of a very special kind, and loads of sensitivity.
He obviously felt a prat about the water & wanted very badly
to make it up to us. He said:

"Let me have a go at this Matt Polly. Come on.
Give me 15 shillings & I'll lose it to him so I can figure out
his system. Then give me all we can afford; and you'll see."

To explain some more about our Ned.
When he plays a game like poker he doesn't try
to figure out what the other players are thinking —
are they bluffing or not, in a weak spot or packing
a good hand. He works out the chances of them
holding certain cards, & does it quick as a flash
while looking like a boy on his first day
at a new school, yeah?

From what Reg had said we'd recognise this Matt Polly
easily. Not only was he as tall as a tree but he had
an eye-patch, like a pirate. Then when Reg's belly was full
& he'd warmed up, he told us the rumour that the patch
covered a socket that had never held an eye: born with
a single peeper, if you please. Now there's a thing.

Off we went to the boozer, Ned perking up.
Getting into the game was tricky. They had to lock
the door of the Snug. Coppers sometimes come in
to the boozer, see.

He loses his 15/- quickly & comes back.
"I know his system. Easy. Can you give me a lot now?

Come oooon."
I gave him more than I meant to, as I was a bit p …
tiddly by then.   He was gone
        for the rest of the evening.
Suddenly we heard shouts from the Snug,
swearing & laughter.
                Then Ned comes back all red in the face
& smiling like a loony.
He'd won very big. What a boy eh?
Then,
                I had a brain wave:
we'll use this dough to buy a motor
& travel to the West Country.
Ned was excited.
Dad not. Just said: "Well that was one in the eye
for lofty."   But he agreed.
& so here we are; full circle, like.
Oh! Talk of the devil. Hello Ned.
Christ! What's up?

Ned has burst into the bar in pyjama jacket
& back-to-front trousers — red in the face
but in quite a different way. Glassy-eyed, almost
terrified, gaping like a fish, trying to speak.
Can hardly get the words out: "D-dad …"

Another facet of Ned is that as a child he used
to stutter very badly & now in late adolescence
it can return if he has an urgent message to pass on
& especially before a crowd. Ed knows this of course
& says in a kindly way: "Sing it Ned" — as stutterers
don't do it when they sing.

Ned gulped, thought hard, gulped, thought hard
& with a face of reluctant release sang:
"I can't wake up granddad

I think he might to de-ead."
Immediately one posho male &
a domino player finished it with …
"*Diamonds are a girl's best friend."*

Four: Dana

Some say attraction switches or grows
or reaches a 'tipping point' (please no!) into love.
Is it really like that?
Don't they have different though adjacent roots?
        Dana's attraction to Ed is strong & steady.
        But, when she sees
him try to put a brave face on the death he'd confirmed
(that was easy: he'd seen enough death in Italy in 1944);
and saying in a failing-breezy way, "well the *I Ching* & Mrs Harpic
never predicted this;" his striving to adopt
a business-like manner; his never meeting her eye
(yet he pats her shoulder); the heart-breaking hug
he gives his distraught son, & his defeated stoop
descending the stairs followed by the boyish straightening up
as if for a fight: then
love seeds itself.   It roots,
sucked nutrient in the night & the next day
lust & love twined around each other to make a rope
tying her to him.

'Only death can sever this', she confides to herself.

Love is also ruthless. Ruthlessly, she's delighted
by Les' death. It's not just her dislike of 'the old lech':
his death will keep Ed here — at least for now. Plus
he will be grateful for all she will be doing for him,
& he can see her in her full glory as an executive
bristling with local nous & respect, vital as spring.

She wonders if he's even noticing her.
He certainly is. Not only that, he wants badly

the comfort of all kinds she can give; but he's paralysed.
The Ed she sees the next day is less touching than touched:
a lumbering zombie, constantly demanding more sugar in his tea,
not leaving the pub, hovering like a rain-cloud in the bar —
too early & too long.   She buys him drinks; he never
thanks her.   It comes to her
that the man she's known till now was the product
of an effort
that's now not being made, showing something of the cockney lout.
It doesn't matter. She's placed in this relation
to him by fate   & that's that.

Meanwhile, Ned's sweetness is beautifully intact.
She finds her eyes turning to him.
She makes sure his dad can see the nurturance
she pours over him.
It's politic & after all there is a *resemblance* minus
the father's current coarse contours.
She fancies she detects jealousy.
She ensures he hears & even sees
the phone-calls she makes on his behalf:
doctor, funeral parlour, solicitor (as if Les had
a Will or even money!), & the trickiest of all —
the Vicar of St Mary's. Could there be a plot
for 'old Mr Hale'?
What luck that Enid Wharton had just been buried
by her daughter in Taunton leaving her shaded niche
by the West Wall going spare. So, 'as it's you dear Dana',
yes indeed.
The funeral will be in two weeks' time.
        A fever of activity descends on her
& it is not *remotely* politic:
it's Love's channelling its fever into the ordering
of a cold tongue & roses, arranging extra staff for
the post-funeral gathering in the Public Bar,
booking a car or cars, posting notices, even back in Richmond.

Dana & Ed collude in the pretence that he
is helping her organise the funeral.
He merely answers questions sloppily
& nods agreement to contradictory options.
"What was Les' favourite piece of music?"
"Oh, the one about roll me over, lay me down
& do it again."   She forces a laugh;
but he is serious.
Gradually, though, he lightens & straightens up,
buoyed by the illusion of agency she gives him.

The day of the funeral is a dream of a day:
feeling like the first day of spring, gorgeously warm & bright.
The church is small, austere, smelling of polish & history.
So cool inside the thickest of walls that anybody
might be persuaded on that day
that the sun through the lightly-stained windows
is not the sun of physics.

Of course, Dana walks in beside, walks out beside,
sits beside & 'supports' Ed, who needs no support.
She looks like she is saying 'bear up old chap';
in fact, she is saying 'this will set tongues wagging, eh'?

Ed does not mean to, but he does
ignore his son; who walks from the church alone,
bravely making no effort to dry his face,
clearly shrunken in spirit.
          However, some effort is made to partner him
in grief by Mr Arnie Scruton, a Mancunian who'd fetched up there
via the Army that spread itself all over Salisbury Plain.
                                        What is he exactly?
He is the main presence behind the bar;
if cooking has to be done (the lock-ins, making or warming,
mince pies etc.) he does it; he
prepares excellent sandwiches & sometimes teas.
He is distinctive: distinctively feminine.

He wears his hair in a fringe over piercing blue eyes,
ever active, ever on a roiling boil of urgent tasks, & ever fey,
delicate & almost squeamish in his movements,
voice soft & high.
He does not 'mince' in his walk & he is not,
in the parlance of the regulars, 'a screamer';
but there is nothing at all manly about him.
He is Dana's sole confidant.

Some regulars call him 'Annie'. & if it's late
will do this to his face, especially if there are other
manly men nearby to share the fun.
Then he hides his upset well, to spill out
when he's alone with Dana.
"Sorry to take on so luv," he'll say.
She thinks of him as her big sister.

So Arnie attempts to guide Ned by the elbow saying:
"He had a good innings son; & what a lovely send-off."
Ned shrinks away, stops dead, leaves Arnie
to walk on alone, unsurprised.

At times like this (there were many)
Arnie would evoke happier times — always times
when it was just Dana & he together.
Lately this was happening often …
When the last drinkers had gone home & they locked up
together, finally sitting before the log-fire embers,
each armed with a large whiskey & soda
while she unburdened herself about Ed …

"What is it about me and men?" she'd say.
"Look at the disaster of my marriage — "

"& your brother's a man too," he'd gently joke.

"Yes he is," she'd reply.

"They fancy me, take what they want from me,
slide away, or deceive, or muck me about, but always
treat me like rubbish … basically."

"Ed's not like that, I can tell. He's as solid as an oak.
I'd only fault him for being a bit dull, frankly."

"Well, I think he's *tremendously* exciting."

"*Chacun à son gout.*"

"So, what should I do Arn?"

"Two things luv. First, make him jealous.
Clearly, & even a touch too much — spur him
to action. Maybe after the funeral at the wake
party here. He'll be here but so will be a lot of
virile farming Johnnies. Second, he's in a stupor
at the mo & so he needs a fire setting
under his bottom.   He won't
make a move on you for yonks, so you'll have
to do something; & in some kind of
extreme situation — but a planned one. If it's routine, like,
he'll just think you're, well, you're *loose*." He giggles.
She hatches a plan. Not routine, but local & possible.

Now, post funeral, the mourners manifest mourning
by drinking, eating, gossiping, the tongue lolling
across a charger lasciviously in a nest of bloody
beetroot & pickled cabbage.
        Dana slips away from him, mindful
of Arnie's advice, set on killing
two birds with one stone:
bird one — aiming for one of the more handsome
youngish farmers, jealousy stimulating;
bird two — farmers know a lot about weather short-term
& she'll pump them for this.

"I wonder Alf, can you suggest a day soon [he gets excited]
when the morning is lovely and sunny but in the afternoon
it rains like Billyo?"

"Ooo … tomorrow, I reckon … you see [*ignored*]. She slips away
again to ask the same thing of Ted, Clive & Rog — same answer
Right, tomorrow it is.   Now she fancies she can feel
Ed's fierce regard burning into her from across the room.
His sad anger turns to joy as she returns
& slips her arm through his.

"How do you feel about a trip up to Stonehenge tomorrow?
I'll pack a pick-nick."   His rapid acceptance,
then his excited bland chit-chat about it being
"a good turn-out" & Les' "making a lot of friends here
in a short time."

"Not among certain husbands he didn't."

The next day Ed makes the mistake of telling Ned about the trip.
"Yeah, that's really good dad. We can have our dinner
sitting on one of those stones."   Dana deals
with this in the following way: shows him her ex-husband's
'racing' bike (a fine Holdsworth) in the shed …
"Now how would you like to ride this
all the way to Stonehenge?"

"Cor, not half. Thanks Miss."

"We'll see you there … Oh by the way, it will take a bit of a while,
maybe most of the morning actually, getting it roadworthy. Here's
what you need. See you for a late lunch then."

Alf, Ted, Clive & Rog were right: a beautiful morning dawned,
in which Ed was surprised by the size of the holdall Dana
had brought the 'pick-nick' in. It remained in the boot
when they wandered among the stones.

She is so relieved
that the spectacle silences his now-irritating excitement.
So relieved he doesn't come out with: 'Can't think
how they got that up there'. Or, 'I wonder what it was all FOR'.
He's calm, cleansed & even elevated, feeling he is centre-stage
in some ancient drama.
All his life
he's lived from week to week (hour-to-hour fighting in Italy)
in one paved & bricked-up jungle clearing or another,
always in a fever of goal-direction, where the future
is no more than a believed-in fiction called up by thrown coins.
Now here he stands among such confidence in how the present
can penetrate the future if not into all time.
Who cares really how they got the stones here or how
they lifted those topping stones & to what end.
That they should do it at all, together, with such poor resources,
& maybe dying in their hundreds
is what counts to him now. It makes the modern world's present
seem tawdry & absurd.
He feels his present-addicted vanity is pulling itself down.
Now he is about
to try to say something about these feelings (even with
his 'poor resources') when there is a thunder-clap
that fulfils the promise of the darkening sky,
followed by a little insinuating rain, followed by pelting
angry rain that stings the face.

"I know where we can go for our lunch … come on."
He follows dutifully as she extracts the holdall from the boot,
takes his hand crossing the main road and makes him
run with her up a track.

It's covered in grass, like a low hillock but obviously man-made
with a metal door in the side.
She is intent & explains nothing,
bends and does something sequential and difficult at the bottom
of the door.

Says sharply:"Give me a HAND!" as she then struggles
to pull open the door of the nuclear bunker.
(These are dotted all over the plane, 'pillboxes'
some call them.)

Leaving the door open she unpacks
the 'pick-nick', which consists solely of a thick rough
blanket & a storm lantern.
"Leave the door OPEN!" sharp again. She strikes a match
to light the lamp & gently closes the door.
Inside, her ash-blonde hair seems as luminous
as this lamp.
The blanket is laid on the ground. Her hair-glow
is in front of, below, above, then in the end beside him.
Now they are both glowing
in the dark beside each other.
This was no pick-nick.

In the silence,
smelling of earth & engine oil, till she speaks:
"Well, that was a bit more thorough than a walk
down the isle followed by an exchange of rings."

"How do you mean?" For him, this is a continuation
of a strange dream.

She explains that she is a 'one guy gal' & that doing
what they have just done "for me adds up to
cementing a partnership— it's like a marriage."

As politely as he can, he raises the fact that she seemed
pretty practiced in gaining access to the bunker, and that
just maybe she's been there before with 'some other geezers …
I mean another geezer … or two'.

She's not offended. Play-punches him. *"You!"*
Tells him that 'a sapper' from the battalion
who used to drink in her pub decided to show a few regulars
'and little old me' how to get in at a period when

'the Ruskies' were threatening.
He swallows his disbelief —
quite happily until she says:

"So … you'll be staying on then, you and the lad.
I'll have to show you the ropes of bar-keeping."
He's too stunned to say more than that he knows them already,
launches into a reminiscence of *The Plough* just to change
the subject, as she leaps suddenly up:

"Neddy! Your poor wet son!"

The rain has eased off quite a bit by now & they later
see Ned riding back & forth on the main road, sometimes
having to stand up to pedal & sometimes peddling furiously
while moving at a snail's pace.
"I think," he shouts, "these dis-railer gears are working
the wrong way round." But he's happy; & they zoom back
to *The Wheel* for lunch. That Ned

is delighted with the plan to stay on helps,
that Ed is sick of discomfort & making do, that
he enjoys being in the pretty village & loves pubs
all help too. But Dana herself helps most of all.
She enchants
Ed's days & nights by deferring to him & yet nurturing him
in the day, by night offering complete compliant abandon
stiffened by some 'I require this' … 'One guy gal'? — he
doesn't dwell on it.

Nothing is announced. They never canoodle or even touch
in public. There's been no obvious change beyond Ed working
behind the bar. Arnie works the same hours; Dana has more
time for 'customer care', plus general enhancement
of the place. & that's not all …
She's determined to add what she calls
'some polish' to Ed. She whisks him off to Salisbury

to have two suits made at Moss Bros along the
'Italian' lines he favours. She's sure his suit shrank
further in that storm. More importantly, she
pretends 'this is for the punters really' but really it's for
her:
"Do you think …
        you could drop the 'boozers, geezers, & bints?'
Do I look like a *bint*? Is this place [she gestures to horse-brasses,
tapped barrels behind the bar, a walk-in fireplace designed
for spit-roasting] a boozer? Is, oh I don't know, Lawrence Olivier
a geezer?"   & as he tries to change such things
he pulls on further threads, finds himself listening
to The Home Service for tips on how to speak.
He takes to it. It works. He talks often in a strange
over-lucid over-emphatic way, like a station announcer.

Talking of Olivier, he's like one of those actors
who get into a part from the externals inwards.
The corrected speech & dress seep into his core;
his orientations & even his dispositions change.
A new kind of manliness arrives: more fatherly towards Ned,
more husbandly towards Dana
(they call each other 'my dear' in private); and so much
has changed that he can play Mine Host with conviction.
It's mocked
by both poshos & yokels behind his back; never to his face,
as he looks too 'handy' for that.

An unexpected & alien contentment descends.
One afternoon at about 3.00 with the lunchtime trade
& clearing up done he wanders out to the car-park
& surveys the front of the pub. L-shaped & whitewashed,
Elegant … How the ground floor is shaded by an awning-like
roof following the frontage round, supported by pillars
to give a cloister effect. It could be, no it is
his palace. This is a domain that suits him, standing
in the blazing sun, hearing birdsong & pregnant silence.

While inside him something boils &
builds the old familiar of: 'this can't be true; what's
ripe must rot. Or will it?
Need to check the *Ching* to find out'.

Ned now has Ed's old room. Ed shoos him out
(Ned had been trying to tune into Radio Luxemburg
on his new transistor) so he can throw
coins in peace.
He locks the door.

"You are funny you know. Your habits.
jingling your change to yourself. Is it a *hobby* dear?"
She mocks him because she'd happened to walk
past the room. She could hear the coins
but not his quiet groans.

He is, says the oracle, a 'traveller' at heart, one of the
dispossessed who's too impatient to settle
on a seemingly comfortable ledge on the mountain
he is destined to climb. If he settles for this he will
'lose his property & his axe'. His *axe*? Ed takes this
to mean something like the 'mojo' that,
unbeknownst to him, Muddy Walters has been
singing about in Chicago for the past two years.

He keeps throwing, hoping for better news &
it's like someone who scratches himself in the full knowledge
it will make the itch unbearable.

"Just popping out to phone mum," he shouts up to Dana.

"Do it here."

"Oh, I've got some loose change I need to use up."

"You and your *habits*."

"Dahrling, I do know a little bit about dear Dana —
from Marie & other contacts around the Plane.
Tread carefully, I would say because — "

"Because she's a a bit of a tart?"

"No, not that. She's a man's woman. Lives through men,
is only able to flourish fully within a man's domain. Or
they're her vessels, if you like. She may well suck you
dry dahrling … if you can bear all these metaphors my precious.
& don't forget — to be dramatic — that Your Goal's Beyond.
Westward Ho! I feel in my old bones that you must *proceed*.
Establish something solid with … er … what's-his-name? … the boy."

Just after he's put the phone down something in him begins
to push back, as against a bully. Why let a few measly coins
& this distant almost indifferent old woman (indifferent to
Les' death too) ruin his first real chance of a home? He makes
a bit more effort with Dana this afternoon: volunteers
to go to the wholesaler, suggest a new range of sandwiches,
gives her little cheek-pecks.

"You're buttering me up … ain't you me old cock-sparrer?"
She's taken to addressing him in cock-er-ney, & adds
"Shan't be raahnd tumorrah" as she skips off to her little car
on some errand or other.

Yes, what if he does move on, leaving her alone?
She's a prize of a woman, for sure.
& could he stomach the thought of her in the arms
of one of the explicit or implicit suitors who float
or floated through the bar or over the rumour transom?
                    Certainly not, in the case of Eugene Honke.
Ed's only seen him once — just before he & Dana
had their pillbox 'lunch'. Swarthy he is, burnished,
a mixture of Jamaican, Jewish, & Portuguese. Dresses
like a top-class bookie, chauffeur-driven in a Humber Hawk,

owns a club in Salisbury; he's rolling in it, rings on his fingers,
patent leather on his toes.
He's loud too, in a silly, self-conscious way, playing up to
& constantly pointing out his resemblance to the leader
of a popular jump-band & novelty combo which is mainly known
for its appearance on The Goon Show — Ray Ellington.
He wanted to call his club *The Bag O'Nails* in homage to Ray's
residence there,
but for copyright reasons has had to settle for *The Sack O'Nails* —
completely missing the tone.

Ominously, Dana has mentioned that he's still 'sniffing round'
since the pillbox. She does dap off to Salisbury very often.
She's a businesswoman who needs capital.   God no.
He imagines himself driving away as she dials Eugene 'Ellington's'
number.

No. He's staying put. 'Be a man'! he finds himself
telling himself. & he's doing just this as he unbolts
the door for the evening trade.
It's not unusual for there to be only one
customer waiting; but for this lone customer to be
Max Tallis is truly shocking.
Max is the kind of guy
who gives bar-flies a good name. He visits this
& other local pubs for company, not drink,
endlessly engaging, & the most quick-witted man
Ed had ever known; never quite literal, always joshing
but never giving offence. 'A word for everybody'
as they say. An answer for everything too.
Yes, he's quick, as flies are. Tall & slim,
seeming to hover
on winged heels from table to table with a joke, an anecdote,
a tease. Never alone; never silent.

But now he gives an entirely earnest "Hello Ed.
Lovely evening."

"All well Max?"

"Not really," Max tells him. His significant other is, or was, a 1950 racing-green Morgan Plus 4 sports car. He's just received the crushing news that it will take more than he can afford to get her back on the road.
"She wasn't old Ed. Let's just say we ran out of road."

"Buy yourself a nice little second-hand Austin 7" … Ed trying to lighten the atmosphere.
He has no come-back except:

"You on your own tonight, Ed?"

Max stays at the bar with his half of bitter, says:
"Where's the boy — Ned?"

"Gone for a ride on a racing bike he's fallen in love with I expect."

"Can I speak freely, given that you're on your tod?"

"OK." This is a new side to Max.

"The whole village knows you & Dana are … fused & that you're here for the duration of what is enduring. But meanwhile what does he do? He's falling back into being a 10-year-old. He needs to be challenged, something to get his brain going."

"He's looking for jobs in the village."

"Butcher's boy, house painter's assistant? It won't tax his brain mate."

"I'm not sure he's got that much of a brain to tax … to be honest."

"To be HONEST! Jesus." Max has changed utterly & in a split second. Now he's a jet of freezing air.
"Are you blind man? He's a bit unworldly & immature,

but Christ does he have a brain on him. The other evening
when it was quiet in here, him & me were going through
these old *Racing Posts* she keeps in that basket by the fire.
Just by looking at the nags' odds over three races against
how they ran he comes up with a system to predict if they'll place.
It's not half bad; & all done in half an hour."

Ed is blushing & ashamed but feels he must defend himself:
"He doesn't know who the Prime Minster is — "

"& lots of morons in this bar do & give their moronic views
on him, while Ned's mind as cool & clear as marble."

A silent Max now watches Ed think.
He's thinking of Ned's chess-mastery, his brilliance in *The Plough*.
Why, he asks himself, did he see these skills as freaks,
as symptoms of a disorder, not islets of excellence that hinted
at a more general excellence?
Yes, blind is just what he's been.

"This is no place for him, old son."

Ed agrees meekly & now stands meekly as Max,
back to his usual self, greets a couple who've just come in —
waltzes the wife round a bit, gets a rise out of the husband
over something football-related. Then he's off,
to leave Ed still thinking about the imprint Max has left.

Yes, they would leave as soon as possible. This decision
pulls more 'threads' in Ed's psyche in the usual way —
about Dana herself this time.
It's been exhausting
having her look at him all the time, with that weird half-smile
that just reveals her rather vampiric canines.
He's been the medium through which her life happens:
Is he enjoying this? What's his take on that? Is he pleased

with her? How is it with 'my man' now?
He suddenly realises
just how much he likes being left alone.
Indeed, he has to admit to himself
        that he sometimes likes being left alone at bedtime too —
        maybe to read the *Express*, which he'd not had a chance
to look at all day, or tune into *The Light Programme* for a bit.
It's unnatural.
With Eunice (his cajoling, her sometimes real reluctance) —
that was more like it, more stimulating.

Yes! They are definitely off. He tells Ned, who's not
particularly upset, as he'd been getting bored.
Ed tells him to keep quiet about it; but he sees the lad
loading all his comics into the boot, plus some jars
of baby beets he's taken a fancy to.
        He overhears his asking 'Miss' if she 'needs'
all the blankets on his bed (he's thinking of upcoming nights
in the car) & if she needs the Holdsworth ('too big for you though')
then he asks his dad if it could be strapped to the roof
of the Standard 10.

Ed tries to tell Tupper in the garage to keep under his hat
all he wants doing to the car, guaranteeing
it will become general knowledge.
                After a few frozen days between them
with zero 'my dears' she shouts down to him from
the box-room she uses as an office. "Ed! Can you pop in?"

She's leaning back on her swivel chair, feet on the desk.
"So, when are you off then Edwin?"

He denies everything as he's not quite ready to leave.
She lists her evidence of car-packing & the rest.
He says things like "well the motor needs new plugs,
sump-change, brakes, you know …"

"It needs new tires, just to potter around here?
It needs new small ends? & I know what Tupper told me.
You pathetic lying toad." The canines are fully exposed now
& the tone is acid-anger.

He shifts from foot to foot, focuses on the wall a foot above
her head & stonewalls & stonewalls
as she swivels from side to side
faster & faster fixing a contemptuous appraising grin.

"There you are. Legs like tree-trunks, the shoulders
of a navvy, you're a blokey, geezery lump me ol cock-sparrer;
but you're a boy, more of a boy even than your son. Weak as water
& passive to the core, ringing mummy to be told what to do.
& that bloody eye-ching or itching or whatever you call it,
that Chinese thing you bored us all with on your first night; you're
consulting that & *that* is what all the jingling behind closed doors is.
You *must* be told what to do.

You think you are fated to fulfil some grand mission —
oh, this is you late at night after a snifter — west of here.
It's not your decision. You have been TOLD it's so.
Has it ever occurred to you that you can know the future
by acting in the present? Of course not. You don't DO.
You obey orders, from the phone-ether, the coins-ether.

What an utter flop you have turned out to be.
I wanted a proper man. Is that so terrible? So difficult?
A bit of male … companionship.
& I get this mild mess of you.
Bonnie. Prince. Charmless."

Now she stops the side-to-side swivel & her eyes narrow,
her voice drops.

"& in the night. What japes, what games. What bloody boredom
of a wet rag. 'Owl jess 'ave a look at ow Fulham go' on on

Saturdaiye, darlin'. & I note while I'm at it that you & Arnie
seem to get on like house on fire. Ever wondered why *dear*?
Or should that really be *ducky*?
Although you pull pints like mining coal you are so dainty
sometimes, so *particular*. So interested in sandwiches, like Arnie.
You call them 'Arnie's sarnies' … God how *fairy* … God what
a wet shit you are."

He replies: "I'll leave you to talk this rubbish to yourself.
I'm sorry to have upset you, but there we are.
Goodbye."

Suddenly she erupts, wailing out torrents of tears.
Stands, sits, stands, sits again, looks up at him
as from under water.
"Don't leave me. DON'T. I love you.
I'll never stop loving you ...
I need you here.   I *love* you."

Then it's as if she tries to roll herself up into a ball
in the chair so she is just hair, body, feet.
He kisses her on the top of the head as you would a child
& tiptoes away, hearing the scream "TRAITOR"
as he shuts the door.

"Anyway, I could have killed him and his son,"
she tells Arnie the next day.
"Can you take it up with him Arn?"

"I'll preVALE on him luv, but I wouldn't hold your breath."
But they have already gone, as Arnie knows.
He can't bear to tell her.

Then she sees & smells his absence, then she finds
an Airtex vest he's left under the bed & at night
cuddles up to it as a child with her comfort blanket,
then it's the total   alteration.

"I've got nothing left to live for Arn," she tells him.

Arnie is scared & can best deal with that by joking:
"Tut tut luv, watch your grammar: you mean you have
nothing *for which to live*." As if that could help.

"I mean it. This is my death. Not my actual death.
I mean the death of my sexual life.
I'm through with men. He was The One & The One
has gone and put me out with the bins."

"You just need a makeover luv. Glam up. Show 'em what they've
been missing. Step OUT!"

"You're half right Arnie." She phones her hairdresser
in Salisbury, *Dickie Beau*.

"Cut it all off Len, short as a man's & dye it a black;
& spike it up."

She washes off her makeup & chucks it all away, buys
dungarees & a boiler suit, checked work-shirts, too big so
she must roll up the sleeves.

"I need your help Arn." She asks him to syphon off
some petrol from her car & to help her gather up
all the bedding Ed has slept in, & to gather up her usual clothes
& underwear, even the specialist underwear — not needing
to keep secrets from him.

She builds a bonfire of Ed-infected cottons & of her female past —
it seems like her past, maybe is her past — in the back garden.

Whoosh!!
She applies a match to some petrol-soaked bras & pillows,
then the flames spread and build.
She nearly collapses as the match-striking evokes her
storm-lantern lighting of a few weeks ago.

Arnie sees through the flames her body wavering like a spirit
in a Hammer Horror — manly in contours only,
so her true sex
comes through all the louder.
She tries to be rough in her movements & decisive sway
& fails in a heart-breaking way.
            He's always loved her

& now in an echo of symmetrical contrast
lust is seeded beside love
& shoots up beside it & twines around it.
He is no longer her 'sister' & they spent
their days & nights together
in a kind of defiant release.

Five: Games

They had left under their own cloud
& are now parked in a layby on the A303 with a lorry
in front of them & one behind them & a van serving
hot drinks, snacks & bacon rolls ahead of all.

"What's 'Bovril' dad? Can I have some?"

"It's not sweet Ned. You wouldn't like it."

"I'll put milk and loads of sugar in dad."

"Can you please just let me read this letter."

As they were about to drive away Arnie had stood before
the car waving his arms.

"Letter for you Ed. Looks official." He was not his
usual self.

"Thanks Arnie … Look after her." He did not reply.

Now he's reading the solicitor's letter:

Young, Shipstead, and Black
Solicitors and Notaries

"Let us take the strain"
Offices in London, Manchester,
Birmingham, Bristol
As from our London Branch
Tufnell Park N19

Dear Mister Edwin Chester Hale,

First of all, may I express my sincere condolences on the demise of your beloved father? Thank you.

Your agent, Mrs Gillespie, as you know, did indeed instruct Pocock and Shaw Solicitors of Salisbury Wilts to endeavour to determine whether your late father Mr Leslie Hawkins Hale had indeed instructed a solicitor to prepare a Will before his timely death. In point of fact, we were the solicitors thus instructed and the aforesaid Will was indeed lodged legitimately with the due authorities in a legitimate manner, enabling ourselves *pari passu* to act as executors *vis-à-vis* yourself.

Thank you for reading this far.

At this time, I now have perforce to be the conveying agent of both "good" and "bad" (*qua* impeding, surprising) news, to wit, that your late father was in possession of a not-insubstantial sum of money, monies to the amount of £8,473, 10 shillings and 4 pence halfpenny, now legitimately lodged with Martins Bank, in the Holloway Road London. That is the "good" news.

I now move to the bad-shading-to-impeding news within the document. While you are indeed the principally targeted beneficiary of the legacy, your father did indeed enter certain conditions upon your receipt of these monies. These are five-fold in nature; and I note that the first four "form a package."

Thank you for reading this far (if you have been).

1. That you should inaugurate, monitor, and legitimately oversee a race of sea-born and sea-going vessels for a minimum of four competitors piloting these vessels, and that you should present the winner of this race with a prize of £100 cash as a reward for their winning the contest. Furthermore, you must provide visual proof of the reward award (e.g., photographic or by cine film), in addition to which the recipient must sign acceptance with their own hand, citing their own address and own date of birth.

2. That you must inaugurate etc. (for the remainder please see above, thank you) a land-born running race along a legitimately-tracked surface for a minimum of four competitors and that you must reward the winner with £100 under the same visual and signatory conditions mentioned in 1…

3. That you must inaugurate etc. (need I say "see above"?) a physical fight with fists encased in leather gloves or not thus encased between two males chosen in respect of in and all due regard to their being the two most competent pugilists encountered by you *sine dubitate* within whichsoever grouping of males you have chosen to encounter for this express purpose. May I take the remainder as it were "as read"? Thank you.

4. That you must, and here I must perforce quote verbatim given the decidedly un-off-the-peg nature of the demand within this interesting nay unique document, "organise a competition between at least two individuals that involves the aiming of fast-travelling, potentially lethal objects at a target." Can I at this point insert a personal reflection? My own mind gravitates to archery and guns; but let us not be stymied by the crabbed imagination of the legal intellect.

5. This final condition partakes of the bad-shading-to-surprising element I adumbrated. It is (a) easier of achievement but (b) perforce requires the total available bequeathed monies to be legitimately reduced to meet the firm's necessary expenses in this instance. That you should visit your father's identical twin brother if he does indeed reside in "the land of the living" at this time. My firm has taken the liberty of determining that Mr Clive Norbert Hale is indeed "alive and kicking" and resident at 12 Quantock Close Severn Beach, Gloucestershire. Our fees will be thereby reverse-disbursed (in the jargon) from the total monies.

Needless to say, in all five cases these visual and signatory evidences must be obtained and in the case of 1-4 the £100 disbursed from your own current financial resources.

You are no doubt asking at this point with regard to the fate of the monies should you fail to bring to fruition any of these five tasks; if, that is you have been reading this far (and if you have, thanks so much). This brings me to another bad-shading-to-surprising element; perhaps more surprising, while recognising of course that this can only be "surprising" should you be *mutatis mutandis* ignorant of the central fact *vis-à-vis* your father. It surprised me, I have to say.

Some years ago, Mr Hale fathered daughters out of wedlock, one whose mother was the popular film actress Margaret Lockwood and one whose mother was the popular film actress Anna Neagle. These two female offspring will by default inherit the legacy, in equal shares.

If indeed you wish to "take up" this challenge may I indeed suggest that you present the aforesaid visual and signatory proofages at one of the offices of YSB. A glance at my map, tells me that our Bristol office may well be that office. If you do indeed decide to "go ahead" you will find the staff at our Bristol branch (Bristol 1) most accommodating, especially Miss Billie Grosswald.

I remain Sir, your humble and obedient servant,

Denis "Archie" Maine, Esq.

A.Maine

(Principal Assistant to the Junior Partner)

Ed immediately gives his son some change
to fetch teas & sandwiches from the van
& roots around for his map.
While Ned is sitting on a low wall chewing thoughtfully
his father thinks desperately; but not for long.

He shouts to Ned to get in, swings the motor
round to go back in the direction they've come from
& soon turns right to take the Shaftesbury Road south.

"We're going to Weymouth Neddy."

"That's sea-side, innit, dad?"

As they drive, Ed explains what's going to be done about
the letter, struggling somewhat around the illegitimate daughters,
wondering at times just how much his son understands
about the facts of life.   He's been expecting

a lot of crazed irrelevance from Ned & the usual
sugar-rush of wrong-end-of-stick-getting, but
apart from ejaculations like: "So we'll be getting a *camera*.
Can we have [a long list of makes]?" ("Box Bownie I think.")
His reactions are more often like

"So do we actually have £400 dad?"

"Thanks to you in *The Twisted Wheel*, yes we do; but only a bit more."

But not much more.

They stop off in Dorchester to buy bread rolls, cheese, & apples
& wandering through the narrow streets
Ned almost begs for one of the advertised 'Cream Teas'.
But when his dad explains again about the money
he falls silent.
This is a new Ned.
Les' absence perhaps has wrought the change.

        It's early in the season so Weymouth is fairly quiet,
while having certain necessities like a funfair on the East Beach
& a Punch & Judy bang in the centre of the esplanade sand.
                The latter keeps Ned amused as his father

takes his bottled-up euphoria to air & release
at the end of the stone jetty on the west side of the beach.
He always feels
like this on coming to the sea; but this is stronger.
It's post the enclosure of Dana's Shrewton & also there is something
about Weymouth itself that he's only felt before in Lincolnshire —
the pure expanse of land & sky that elevates & expands you rather than
making you feel like an atom in the vastness. Mainly, though,
it's from being just where he is at the end of the stone jetty.
British surrealism
was mostly a dowdy affair, with giant sea shells
in the wrong places, society ladies with chiffon scarves
occluding their faces, & ventilation funnels
springing up like mushrooms. *Somehow*
this is all here, plus an echo of Popeye
& the old sailor on packets of Player's cigarettes.
In a word: it is a waking dream he stands in,
not wanting to leave it today,
happy to stand there for ever.

Later he fetches Ned & they go off to buy a Box Brownie camera,
a roll of film, a writing pad, & some biros. Armed with these
they look for a pub — not to drink in particularly, but
for potential competitors.

"It's perfect!"

"What is dad?"

"Never mind."

Yes, it does feel perfect to him —
the harbour essentially *behind* the beach,
like a backstage area
& over all
the heavenly aromas of the brewery at the sea
end of the harbour near the Nothe Fort.

Also perfect is the old salt renting rowing boats
by the hour & an orange buoy out to sea
towards Portland Bill, easily visible from
the jetty's end.

"Let's see the colour of your money boss?"

Yes he is cheeky but … Ed shows the lad the five £20 notes
in his wallet. Another of the lads
quickly says "You're on!"
They're from the Midlands & probably on
their first pint & the best I can do
is to identify them by hair.
The cheeky one has a crew-cut; the keen one is
ginger; one has blonde hair; & one has black curly hair.

Ed pays for the hire, one boat each of course.
He tells them they have to row round the buoy &
first back into the harbour wins the money. The winning post
is a capstan. Ginger & Blonde are happily raring to go,
Curly-black is nervous but determined; crew-cut seems not to give
a toss & is smoking steadily.

The 'old salt' abandons his act lapsing into cockney to say …
"Quid extra per boat if they're racing, guvnor," as he sees them
lining up the prows to start. "Local regulations & all that mate."

"Shut up you!" says Ned who has just had
his first ever half-pint of bitter.

Ginger & Blonde set off at a furious pace watched by people
taking tea in the Nothe Fort Gardens. Curly-black is striving
to keep up but his oars slip often from his sweaty hands.
Crew cut seems to be out for a quiet jaunt on a sunny day,
lighting fag from fag, sometimes waving to the tea-takers.

Ed can see clearly, stationed at the end of the jetty,
that Ginger & Blonde are getting their oars entangled
rounding the buoy, & doing so drift out to sea flailing slightly.
Seizing his moment, curly-black tries to slip between them
& and the buoy causing one of his oars to bang into the buoy
& fall into the water. In fact, this makes him level with
the two front-runners as they too have lost an oar each
in the entanglement.

"First one to give me an oar lads," says Ginger, "& I'll split
the hundred with them."

"Sheet-face!" the blonde & curly-black say almost in unison.

Crew-cut gives his three cussing angry mates a wide birth
rounding the buoy
& rows slowly home, smiling to himself.

Ned is very excited to be in the photo handing over the money
to Denny Osborne of Walsall. Who, after doing the required writing,
tells Mick Farron of Wood Green (a sea salt) that he'll split the payment
for the oars with Ed.

That was easy, all too easy; so easy Ed's dreamlike feeling returns.
He supresses this by taking Ned to look for a secondary school.

"Can you tell me if there is a secondary school nearby?
It must have a playing field attached."
The woman in the Tourist Information Office has never heard
this one before & simply says: "Sorry, no." & then, as they
are about to leave, adds suddenly:
"Would you by any chance be from Candid Microphone
on Radio Luxembourg?
I mean are you Jonathan Routh at all?"

A young man sorting leaflets on a display overhears this
& says "St Brendan's on the Portland Road [he gives directions].
Ask for Jock Mooney — the mad bastard."

Ed decides he needs a walk & Ned needs to let off steam,
so he goes alone, leaving Ned to look for two cheap pairs
of swimming trunks.   The walk & the dull generics
burn away his dreamt state till he sees:

St Brendan's Academy
Head Master: Mr John Mooney (Dip.Ed. Redland)
"God moves in mysterious ways"

"So … a *hundred* poonds ye say … "

Ed struggles to keep a straight face as he explains
how his late father had a deep interest in athletics
& the sport of running especially, when in fact
his own running interests were confined to swift exits
at the approach of husbands.

"Now, it is rather a large sum tae give tae a wee *youth* …
Er … maybe the optimum strategy is to *present*
it tae the winning laddie in the *expectation* that it will be
transferred into the *safe keeping* of the academic authorities —
for the *nonce*."

Ed & the rogue understand each other.
His office resembles a police station interrogation room.
The metal desk supports no more than a telephone & the shelves
support no more than selection of canes &
black-board-rubbers (for throwing, mainly). Though this is
a police station in a black comedy starring Bob Hope.
Mooney's ultra-neat black greased hair is far thicker
than Hope's, but otherwise the resemblance is remarkable —
which he knows & plays up to.
                He has no wisecracks,
but is given to making sour or joshing remarks
in a wisecracking style — side-jutting Hope-like jaw
& a twinkle set in his eyes.

This know-nothing's reign of terror
began a year ago after Father Beverley O'Neil
left under a cloud. Mooney had picked up some maths
in the army along with a suite of sadistic habits …

"Aye well, 4A & 4B have games tomorrow between 10.00
& 12.00 so come at 10.30 & we'll have 'em race for ye."

There was no Goodbye. He just picked up the phone
& told his secretary to bring him tea,
plus a bun & 20 *Senior Service*. After a night

in the car they are stiff & tired.
The weather is dull, threatening rain. Mooney
walks up to Ned, his face inches away &
simply Hope-juts his jaw in a silent wisecrack.

"I'll have a wee wurrd wi' the Almighty & the rain
will hold off." Looks around for laughter among the boys
& there'd better be some … "Feeling a bit down
in the dumps are we Jarvis?
Would ye like something
tae be depressed *aboot*."
He twists the boy's ear till tears start.

The weather does not prevent Ned from spending
the last of his money on a double ice-cream cone
with clotted cream & a raspberry squirt. There are
only six in the race: the best four runners, Paine,
Truss, Conway, & Shapps & two mediocres.
It will be over 880 yards.

As it starts, Ned is uncontrollably excited
having eaten half of the ice quickly on an empty stomach.
"Cut across Shorty!" he shouts as he sees Shapps fall
behind from the three front-runners. In doing this he waves
his arms & in doing that the ice goes flying onto the track.

Here's Paine rounding the final bend only 40 yards
from the tape.
Here's Paine slipping on Ned's ice
to starfish himself on the ground.
Here's him grounded seeing his hated rival Truss cantering in
to win & here's Paine
sticking out a leg to trip him
as his best mate Mick Conway, once in third place, enjoys
an easy win.

Mooney is delighted with this outcome as it gives him
a chance to announce the winner of the race
to the assembled boys in the following way:
"I hereby declare the winner to be this twit Conway."
Then a Hope-jut & scan of boys as they force laughs.
They have all heard of Conway Twitty's current chart-topper.

This does not remove the delighted grin from Conway's face;
but whatever Mooney whispers at length to him certainly does. All
of which
makes Ed's photographic proof a strange affair:
a downcast presenter Ned (his ice-cream-loss),
a downcast recipient Conway (Mooney's mits
on his winnings), with Mooney beaming between them
like a politician who has just brokered a peace deal
between two loser states.

"What was dad/granddad thinking?" is in their minds
as they drive away. Ned feeling a fool, Ed feeling
like a tacky pragmatist shading into the enabler
of a nasty crook, & for what? A ridiculous photograph
& a scrappy bit of paper torn from an exercise book.
They are silent, both wanting this charade to end.

The next task is the trickiest & most dangerous —
getting two tough men to fist-fight … Well,
Ed has some ideas.

Between the long finger of the 'backstage'
harbour & the classic English seafront of sun-tan & saucy postcards
exist pockets that are dank & dark. The streets are narrow
& in those streets are pubs that are not just tourist unfriendly:
white-collared men shrink away from them & women
pull their children away from the very street.
Walking past you might hear
'OGGY OGGY OGGY OI OI OI' chanted by the whole pub.
Men will normally be stationed at the door,
not to discourage undesirables
(they're encouraged!) but to look out for coppers.

One of these (*The Turtle & Spigot*) also has a small car park, never used,
because who would leave his car unattended *there*? They wait for it
to fill up (builders from a nearby site plus a fair number of free-floating
hard-nuts).
Ed has the clear advantage
of being strong & fearless. He always was, but the war has amplified it.
While his son is a terrifying fighter when angry & his threshold
for anger is low right now. They don't expect trouble.

"Can I make an announcement?" he asks the barman.

"Keep it short."

"Hello everybody! For reasons it would take too long
to go into I'm offering £100 to the winner of the first fist-fight
to take place in the car park in the next half hour.
Any takers? £100! Come on lads."

Various cries —

"Oggy Oggy Oggy! Oi Oi Oi"

"Cockney wanker!"

& most to the point …

"Wassa catch then?"

"Only that you have to have your photo taken with the dough
& sign to say you've received it … £100 chaps!"

There follows five minutes of unfriendly chaos & hilarity then cries of …

"Ter! Wherrs Ter got to? He in the bog or what? Get him.
Get up yer Ter."

Terry French steps forward doing air punches & grinning.
He's the flyweight champion of Dorset, like a single
twitching muscle surrounded by a *Ready Brek* glow of meanness.

"Give it to I mate. Better do.
They knows I can beat the shit outa anyone yer.
Better give it to I." A clever-dick pipes up:

"Better give it to our Ter. Don't wanna be 'sponsible
for some sod's brain damage, do you London?"

At this point, Ed pauses for thought. He would
rather avoid the whole squalid business & just get
the photo & signed page. It's no more dishonest than
the race fiasco.
Then a low voice from the back of the room:

"Hang about!"

"We forgot about Fat Frank." More hilarity.

Frank Coggins is old & quite fat, but he was once
a fearsome heavyweight. His knees click as he slowly stands,
but once standing towers over even Ed — he moves like
Frankenstein's monster.

"OK." says Ed, & so does Terry.

In the car park Frank's role is the taker of punishment (cut eye,
split lip, breathless from a belly blow, made giddy by his own
reckless missed punches); though, if any of his hooks and jabs connect
"our Ter" will be in trouble.

Frank slips or is pushed over. It had to happen.
But then something else happens — to Frank.
He is furious with himself & channels his fury onto his opponent.
Now he's fast but manically so, fast & wild, a cartoon tank with fists,
something between a bear & a tank, a bear maddened by hornets.
        Again, it had to happen — Frank connects
        with Terry's jaw, the crack loud enough
to be audible above the spectators.
It's over.

The flyweight is now off to the cottage hospital —
in a bad way.
The crowd's rumbling anger had to happen too;
        Father & son are tremendously satisfied.
They don't seek violence, but they love fistfights — first
or third person. They like their honesty. But mainly,
it's the sensual thrill of them.
                It turns out that
Frank Coggins lives in a hostel, so he needs the money.
Excellent. The crowd gives him plenty of space now.

"Let's get some fish & chips Neddy." He almost adds: "to celebrate."
They eat them on the front, having first put their jackets in the motor —
it's so hot. Ed fancies they are being watched
by some of French's supporters.
He's correct.

Air riffles, the ones at the fair down the beach. He'll have to arrange
something there. Will they do? Are air-riffle pellets
'potentially lethal objects…'
Not meaning to, he muses aloud:

"You could kill someone if you fired an air-riffle into their eye."

Ned, thinking he is addressed, contemplates a long drooping chip …
"Nah, just brain damage dad. Won't even bleed to death."

"But they might die of the shock — heart attack, with a bit of luck"
At which they collapse laughing.
        Just then a motorcyclist narrowly avoids
        crashing into a young family.

"I have an idea,' says Ed.

When they reach the fair, Ed makes for a low wooden tower
with a toll-booth at the bottom & steps up to a viewing platform
circling the rim of the in-fact-hollow tower. Here people gaze
rapt over the edge down into the tower while there is an angry
but rhythmic roar from within it, like a sighing dragon.

It's the Wall of Death,
It's the Roar of Death,
It's splendid.

Yes, death does loom for the motorcycle rider
who overshoots the rim or whose engine cuts out.
The wooden pit is the round hole into which a round peg
would fit nicely. There are two riders there, taking it in turns
to put their trust in centrifugal force. One rides while
the other smokes.   It's shocking
        just how close to the edge they come to thrill
& scare the watchers & how soon they pick up enough speed
to ride horizontally up & round the wall.

The rider does not just circuit the sides like a ball-bearing
swirled in a cup: there is an element of 'razzle-dazzle 'em'.
He swoops up from the base seeming to aim (or actually aiming)
for particular viewers.   Exactly here
is the essence of the Wall of Death's glory. One looks down

at the rider's face
coming up to you like a surfacing fish
& on that face there is such a fear-full concentration
that touches the fear you feel as his target.
Exactly this was the experience of father & son.

"Bloody hell dad!"

"Don't swear Ned."

As I say: two riders. One is short & tubby, a fag always on the lip,
only leaving it at the climax of the wall-climb. He is the one who's
more of a mechanic, tinkering with the very low, silencer-less
machine now & then. He's like a sleepwalker. The other
is what Les would have called a 'lascar' — an Indian
of the seagoing type. Such men often have handlebar moustaches &
this chap has a splendid one, plus a fez fixed to his head
by an elastic strap. He's all chats and smiles
at his silent colleague. But how
to talk to them, when they seem so distant locked
within the pit universe?

"Can I have a word?" Ed shouts down between lulls.

Tubby wants to be seen to ignore this, but lascar replies.

"Come down. Knock side door. One tirty."

This gives him half an hour … But what can the 'target'
of their 'potentially lethal object' be?
His pondering is frequently interrupted by Ned's bubble-popping,
for Ned is addicted to bubble gum and bubble-blowing.

"Ned, give me that gum."

"But daaad … "

Ed squashes carefully the pink blob about three inches below the rim —
just a shade above the highest black tyre mark near them. The first rider
to touch the gum with a tyre wins the money.
Yes they're more than happy
to take this on — this job pays peanuts. They toss
for who goes first. It's the lascar.
Nope, he's well short;
Tubby a bit nearer, lascar shows no improvement; Tubby
nearly does it … & then lascar is bang on target. Ed runs his finger
delightedly along the imprint of the tyre on the pink blob; after which
all goes smoothly with photo & document: Mr Ashok Modi
is the winner. Tubby pats him on the back.

Then they & the other watchers watch as Ashok gives
half the money to Tubby, causing that rare thing —
a smile from him. Surely this smile is about more than money.
At this moment
Ed feels his heart will burst from happiness. Has it,
he wonders, been his father's design to have him experience
hells & heavens?

"Come on Ned. We'll toddle up to Dorchester &
you can have one of these cream teas."

It's obvious from a distance:
all four of the tyres have been slashed.
Inside the car
it smells of rubber — because a fire of rags has been set
beneath it. Of course it doesn't start.

On the windscreen a scrap of cardboard with the words:

TERRY SHOULD OF
WON IT SHITBAG!!!
FROM
THE IPA CREW.

The next 'heaven' now feels beyond everything.
It feels non-existent.

'IPA'? It takes no thought; his mind goes there in
milliseconds. Ioanna Panagiotidou — I P & A.
Certain it's short for that.
Got to be.
It all makes sense now.
She must have worked with those solicitors: the promise of money
that's impossible to get hold of & her yobbos around the country
to make sure of it.

Ned cannot recognise his father when he's like this,
with the rigidity of a tin soldier & the feyness of a teenage girl.
He is embarrassed
when Ed shares his firm convictions about Ioanna;
but it braces the lad.

"Tell you the truth dad, I think this is rubbish.
Do you remember when you bought me that beer
& I said Can I have IPA as I'd seen it on a pump?
You said it was too strong. Dunno what IPA is though."

"It's 'India Pale Ale' son … Oh … I don't know."

In fact, he does know: he should at least *try*
to snap out of it.

"Phone granny."

"OK."

But first he phones a garage, who say they will come the next day.
They spend the day on the beach & go for a swim.
At least they try to swim, wading half way to France
before the water is waist-high.

"Margaret *Lockwood*!!!!

Anna Neagle I can almost believe
but that he cracked *her* … "

Vera has been silent up to that point, grunting every so often
to tell him she was listening to the long Will-&-tasks saga.
There is less animation in her off-the-peg advice:

"Just get ON with it dahrling. I know, I just know
that when you get to the right region of the West
you & … Thingie will sew the seeds of a brilliant —
what to call it? — Empire that will benefit all mankind.
Go where you have to & do … blah blah blah.
Ioanna is a figment, candy-floss on a stick you've made.
Get HOLD
of the old sod's money — as if it was ever his.
& never ever forget that mummy loves you.
Keep in touch … Must dash, bridge with the Fitzgeralds
tonight." She nearly adds:
"& DO grow a backbone dahrling."

The man from the garage sucks air in through his teeth (as
they do)
& lies that the IPA Crew have put sugar in his tank …

"Tell you what I'll do for you mate. You say you can't
manage the 150 nicker to put it right. Well [tooth suck]
I'll give you 30 quid to take it off your hands & a lovely
nearly-new Lambretta — young chap couldn't keep
the payments. Beautiful blue, loads of storage on her for … eh …
your stuff."

Ed accepts a lift to the garage & picks up
the admittedly-pretty-stylish eggshell-blue scooter
& the much-needed money.
At any other time he would have enjoyed riding her
back into town. Meanwhile Ned

has palled up with some lads of his own age & is playing
football (with a tennis ball) in the car park of a pub.
I cruelly said at the start he was a 'seal' ... He has
the buoyance of one. He lifts his dad's heart.   This,

& the need to focus on the practicals, helps to combat
the furious passion of his theories.   What to keep,
what to jettison? Should he get a provisional bike licence?
(No, that means he'll need an L-plate & learners can't take passengers;
he'll have to watch out for coppers). What do they do now
their four-wheeled bedroom has gone? But mainly he is
marvelling at his son.

A fine rain falls just as they are about to head north-west.
It has to be said that these two hefty men on a scooter
wearing pack-a-macs & those little grey transparent caps that
they come with do not look like Empire-founding warriors.

Six: Hell

"Be quicker to walk mate."

"Can I give you a lift?"

— throaty jeer —

"Wanna push?"   These

are some of what they hear from hitch-hikers
by the side of the road.   It's
the men's weight, the full panniers, the enormous rucksack
on Ned's back, the precious little duffle bag at Ed's feet.
They'd left too late & so Ed decides
they'll have to fork out & stay the night in Shepton Mallet.
                To hell with it:
if they'd been on time they would have had a cream tea there.
They need a 'lift'.   Sitting by the stone cross
in the marketplace they simultaneously decide on a drink,
find a pub in a side-street that's also a B&B — try
to suck back some good from the day.

"Let's have one of those 'wash & brush ups' dad."
He's seen them advertised (a few pence for one
in some Gents) but really he feels, like his dad, they need
a spiritual version of just that.

Having had
the best night's sleep in months, a bath, & a fried breakfast,
they arrive — after tortuous striving up Mendip Hills —
in Bristol.   They see "Centre" signposted,
& in Baldwin Street, *en route* to it, a Labour Exchange.
Ed tells Ned to try to get a live-in job (hotel, pub, nursing home …)
& that he'll see him in the centre of the Centre at 6 o'clock.

"First to the solicitors, then to this Clive character. Now where's
the Brownie & the exercise book …"

The second his son's substantial rear-end disappears
behind the double doors
he feels coldly alone.   Bristol seems fine,
but what if it's all a gigantic folly? What if … sod it.

The centre is one big roundabout with *The Hippodrome*
theatre at the hill end, the docks end on the left and in the centre
of the roundabout
public toilets; but also
an invitingly empty space & a statue of somebody.

Surprised to see a number of scooters
like his near the statue
attended by, hovered around by, a group of young guys dressed
& coiffured like himself, though half his size. They look
at him in a puzzled-appreciative way.

"Allroit mate?"

"Hi there. Do any of you happen to know where I can find
Young Shipstead & Black solicitors?"

"You down from London then?"

So odd to him to hear yokel speech in the mouths
of men who look like Soho coffee-bar cowboys, talking about
having a 'noyce toyme' & saying 'yer, give it to I then'.

"Jew ever go to jazz clubs up there then?"

"Yes I do, used to."

Yes he did. He doesn't like rock & roll, likes French pop music,
& modern jazz. All mocked by Les, with 'boopiboppipoo
bappidoody' etc. with 'say bopperebob Daddy's got a beebob'.

A brief chat about 'Charlay Parker' & they try
to pump him about the West-End clubs & R&B;
but he must find YS&B soonest.

"Oh yeah, sat bo'um'u Christmas Steps. Over thur.
Don't go up near the Cawston Hall, go on to
Broadmead. Can't miss it."
They won't let him get away
until they've told him about the Chinese Jazz Club
in the Corn Exchange & the cellar club under Carwadines
('bit of R&B but fuckin' trad an all').

He leaves his scooter near theirs
& heads off in the right direction ("Cheery-boi" they say).

So *this* is Christmas Steps.
Narrow, steep, Medieval? Feels like Fagin & his troupe
could come cantering down any minute.
Four or so stone, platformed flights with bijou shops on either
side, more of an alley than a street.
So dark. Stagey, & yet like a deep fissure
in a cliff face.
Irrelevant to me all this, he tells himself.
Ah! Here's YS&B.

The atmosphere in the place is strange indeed.
It's not particularly hot but there are three electric fans
full on making blinds clatter & lifting papers from desks.
Here's a desk behind which 'Miss Billie Grosswald' sits.
Round, middle-aged, very flustered, but friendly-effusive.

Suddenly it hits him: he's forgotten to get the photos developed.
Almost in one breath he explains who he is & why he's here.
Billie listens with her head on one side, rifling through papers,
passing her hand across her forehead as if in a heavy sweat.

"Old Pete Thomas up Christmas Steps will do them for you
in a couple of hours. He runs the *Joke Shop*, but develops
snaps too. You have time for a nice cuppa at *The Hundred Shafts*."

Here she winks. Surely not at a sexual pun.

"It's opposite the *Joke Shop*. Half-way up.
Just leave the signed documents here … hmm
I'm impressed, nice job …
God it's stuffy in here … The Boss Old Mister Young's
son was in earlier, quite threw me off … talk about 6s & 7s.
See you soon Mr uh Hale. Enjoy *The Hundred Shafts*
[another wink]."

Pete Thomas emerges from among the displays of black-face
soap, itching powder, false noses, & 'artistic' photographs
of athletic women with big breasts & thighs. Yes, for a huge
fee, they will be ready at 1.30.   Ed is intrigued

by the tiny pub called *The Sugar Loaf*, a little clothes shop with
items carefully arranged as for an exhibition; a pair of herring-bone
bell-bottoms in the window, plus two pairs of Levi jeans. & here's
The Hundred Shafts 'Hot drinks, continental cakes & biscuits,
herbal cigarettes'.

Is that Mose Allison playing when he walks in?
The inside is far bigger than he expected, knocked through
to next door & knocked up to the floor above, cave-like.
He cannot take it in.   This is only part of
what he cannot take in —
the clientele falls into three clear groups:
beatniks with long matted hair & goatees wearing
black pullovers, talking in low voices, drinking tea;
continentals, rather like the guys on the Centre
but certainly not working class, drinking espresso, smoking,
or eating delicate pink biscuits with fine chocolate latticework,

their conversation rapid & narrative;
& a group of guys who are probably
University students but also some kind of club —
dressed almost identically in tight well-cut suits of ginger tweed
& high-healed boots, white open-necked shirts
with wide collars &, strikingly, all with one hair-style —
a neo-Regency style, longish & brushed forward at the sides,
quiffed up at the front, Romantically tousled. They can easily
be heard to be discussing philosophy
or history in their measured drawls. They smoke
herbal cigarettes.

So here is Ed, standing at the counter.
There are few women customers (none with the Regency gingers),
but all have long straight hair, mostly parted in the middle
making curtains through which their heavily-made-up eyes peep.
This style
is favoured by the pretty girl serving (upper-class, dreamily
disdainful). He doesn't know what to order.
Behind
the counter: an array of herbal cigarettes in beautiful pastel shades
along with some, new to him, cigarette brands like *Passing Clouds*
& some *Black Russian*; an espresso machine (no froth available);
a blackboard with the names of teas he's never heard of.
He feels
adventurous. This place stimulates it, with its smoky sweet odours
& cool music. He feels he has been allowed to enter the domain
of very exclusive tribes — of future people.

All the teas are expensive & one of them is by far the priciest —
'aya' at nine shillings eleven pence per cup. It must be special &
this moment is too. I'll go for that, is his thought.

"What's so special about the aya?" He asks the girl.

"Don't you know about it? It's what we call a feel-good tea.
Better steer clear of it though if you're not feeling A1.
Then it's feel-bad." Said with not the flicker of a smile.

"I'm fine. I'll go for that."

"Sure?"

"*Sure*!" He's trying to impress the girl.
Now
this is the edge-of-the-wedge between
what is the case
& what Ed knows & feels about it,
especially feels.
This wedge will of course
widen as we progress till finally it will dissolve
& he is back home in the reality of the upper air.

'Aya' is short for ayahuasca:
a Peruvian plant whose effect is similar to, though milder than,
mescaline. How it affects the imbiber depends
upon the mental buoyancy of the imbiber. Unlike
the 'herbal' cigarettes sold under the counter
or in the back room, aya is legal. In any case,
the police are naïve, not tolerant. Yes,
the beatniks look like 'drug fiends', but they can only afford
bitter — not 'reefers'.

"Oh, & a custard slice please."

"A *Mille-feuille*, certainly."

He just cannot believe how much of their precious resources
he is handing over; but something in the moment is pressing
him to do it. He sits,
The music changes.
An alto sax
swinging like crazy;
but maybe about to crack
at any second.
Almost unpleasant, almost, this tea
metallic, bitter; & is the alto tone too?

Thank the gods for this meal-flow or whatever she called it.
Drums his fingers & taps his feet, head back smiling.

"Art Pepper" says one of the Continentals near him.
He drinks the rest of the brew as the music changes again.
He used to fidget.
He's not fidgeting now.
Decides to count the flaky crumbs
left from his messily-eaten cake … 49. 'Revolution'
in the *Ching*. Excellent! But hasn't two hours gone already?
It can't have done. It has.

He collects the photos from Pete Thomas, failing to stop himself
buying a plastic dog turd as a present for Ned.

"Aren't these lovely snaps?" says Billie. "Don't worry
because one of them is of a darky, It'll go through head office.
Trust me. Now here's Clive Hale's address. Suggest you catch
the local train from Temple Meads up to Severn Beach.
Go up Baldwin St then over Bristol Bridge."

"Temple Fortune?"

"Temple *Meads* … But look, be careful out there dressed
in that continental way & with your accent.
You need to watch out for Teds & Gowners."

"Gowners?"

"You'll get to hear about them soon enough.
Advise you to steer clear of North-West Bristol —
Henbury especially. Look after yourself.
See you anon & *bon courage*."

This is what she said & it was also what he heard;
but this is what he understands by it:

"You & the Gowners will be the source of
a river of foaming human blood. Strife & penury are your
immediate lot. Rape & revenge the theme-tunes. You think
you can force Ioanna back into your unconscious mind
as if she were
a chimera or false belief, force back like pressing into
a waste bin a rotting fish-head. She is the prime mover
of desperate war & your need to conquer, shedding bloody blood,
to avenge vile arrogance & lust.
Yes, you'll find a home at last,
but only in blood-soaked earth. Irony piles up,
with Greeks lending support in a tainted fate.
Don't give up. You'll win a local bride.
Above all, prize your son. RICHLY. Your
glorious son."

The chemical ministry of aya works to set him apart
from both good & bad phenomena, in a stoic style.
He's cold. He is not strong but castellated. Within his
castle he in inclined to say:
"Fair enough, Miss Grosswald. Let's pass on now.
Don't I know this already? I've forgotten.
Now where did I leave my horse or Lambretta?"
"See you later," is all he says.

"Giddy up!" He finds himself saying to the scooter
as he tears down Baldwin St to Temple Meads.
Approaching the bike park at the station
he says to it:

"Wo Trigger!" He dismounts, patting it on the petrol tank
saying: "A fine piece of bike-flesh."

Of course he knows he's not normal. He's watching what
will happen next, watching abnormally.
The steam hiss & acrid smell.
The huge black flanks & warlike wheels

of the trains are all refreshing
after the soft hours
of Shrewton & Weymouth. But it's a mile from him.
Near him is the thought

that these monsters
are transporting refugees
against their will,

the station staff prodding & threatening.
He sees a little man break away from a cowering group
in an escape attempt, sees him halted by a small angular robot
of enforcement, sees him return to the group
with a package of fresh impediments …
& he see all this dispassionately as if it were a feature film.

What he actually sees
is a family travelling on the *Flying Scotsman* to Glasgow,
their 10-year-old son being given sixpence, his going
to a dispensing machine to buy a red & yellow box
of chocolate raisins, and his satisfied return.

On the distant local platform things are more manageable.
He sits in the compartment of a corridor-less train until
an old lady joins him carrying a cat in a basket.
Who is making her do this? He asks himself.
Why must she carry a cat, this turbulent evil spirit?
She tries to engage him in conversation &

"Well, *this* is a day of days!" is all he bats back.

She politely interprets this as a weather report.

"Yes, it is indeed overcast."

Everything changes when they reach
Filton Abbey Wood Station's

thronged platform with high-spirited day-trippers.
The lady leaves & two families (friends) get in:
both with young children; loud & excited (the parents too).
The wives tease their husbands good-heartedly
about their true motivation for coming (the licencing
hours in Severn Beach are liberal & it is advertised
even in London as 'The Blackpool of the West').

Ed understands little of what is being said back & forth.
Partly, it's the accents, mainly it's what he's caused to
understand of it by the fatal mixture of aya & mind.
He hears the wives charge their husbands with
physical & moral impotence & DIY incompetence;
he hears the men fight back weakly ending every sentence
with 'arr mum'; the children's laughter is
shrieks of despair at the tragedy of it all.

"Why are they so alone?" something says to himself.
"Who makes them do this? Who could ever
ENJOY this."   He wants to say

"How can it be a *beach*!
We're travelling UP the estuary.
There IS no beach.
Why not stay home a drink a bottle of best bitter
in your coalhouse!" But says instead:

"Now *this* is a day of days."

"You alroit pal?"

He closes his eyes
on a red field & feels
the train move forwards chuffingly,
swooping down like a big dipper,
but stutteringly.

Cement.

The first impression is of cement, a crabbed little field
of it & a cement-grey foreshore.
Bolted
to the cement are "rides" often with "Whizz"
or "Wheezer" or "Manhattan" in their names
& little queues of children clutching their pennies.
There are three pubs,
prefabricated, spilling
onto the "pleasure beach".
On each table outside them a transistor radio,
often playing different stations loudly & un-tuned.

Ed loves
birds & thinks they are the most beautiful
creatures on earth. The — he cannot decide on how
to think about it: foreshore, riverbank? — is rich
in birds dipping, bobbing & picking their way. They flee
from him. None
fly over the 'pleasure beach'. In Italy
he loved how jays would scavenge
from café tables so he could watch their ways
& feathering up close. These birds,
he decides,
are disgusted by the cement field,
the bolted rides in feverish colours,
the dangerous laughing of tortured agents.
Imagine one of these birds
floating in the centrepiece —
the *Blue Lagoon* swimming pool,
this 'sea' of the 'beach'. A sea trapped
within ultramarine tiles & chrome steps.

About all this, Ed is as dispassionate as ever
but tormented in intellect that none of the people
seems to know, not really *know* that
there is no beach.

It's a frightening fact to him.
Why?
The place is really not so bad:
tacky yes but people are getting together,
letting off steam; it's jolly.
        For Ed,
        all this is a sign of lifelessness:
the death of truth;
an alienation from reality
(this from a man a mile from it).
It's lively to them but dead to Ed.
Why?

To think that naming it makes it so.

Call it a 'beach' & it *is* a beach & people
will ignore their senses
stupidly alone against the authority of given
words —
in the blind stupor of an imposed real.
Yes, he will tell them individually —
if only he had a loud hailer —
that there is NO BEACH.

He goes up to one of the pub tables
shouting over their radio, finding himself saying:

"Do you know where I can buy a guide to
Severn Beach please?"

At this an uproar of laughter, even
from the kids.
But a granddad figure says:

"Only 'guide' we know of is Sharon
at the *Blue Lagoon*."

"Yeah, try arr Shar!" they shout.

"We charges, we have a SURcharge for patrons
on their own. Don't you have a famlay?"

Ed tells Sharon that he wants to find
Quantock Drive.   She speaks,
but he is transfixed by the *Blue Lagoon*.
What are these creatures in the water
with the bodies
of otters & the heads of children?
What scientist did this to them?
Who forces them to live in water
that's like mouthwash. Why are they in mouthwash
& will the transistors ever fall silent?

"Can you say that all again please?"

"For half-a-crown I'll draw you a map."

"OK"

Ten minutes later …

Severn Beach suburbia is tiny, but for Ed this
is as big as Wembley, as Whitton, as Hounslow,
while being the central tendency
of them all.   It was bad before.
It's truly hellish now.

Against this
        the Pleasure Beach is Heaven.
        These tortured agents were alive.
But this is what is done, by way of thoughtful torture
after they die.   Hell is not
being alone forever; it's not
being squashed up against the wrong people forever;

it's being walled around forever in a space,
especially a large space.
& whether or not with other people,
& being *defined* by that unmoving space:
that's Mr Sampson
that's Mrs Chaundry
that's the Marshalls
that bit of land, these bricks & tiles are *you*.

See how each space [this is all in Ed's mental language
un-articulated] is painfully distinguished from nearby others.
What goes through a man's mind as he is painting his half
of the top of a fence a different colour to his neighbour's side
(a drainpipe even), maybe
watching the paint blister in the sun
or be pocked by rain … 'Is this line straight Marjorie'?
The plot is you & together with other ex-agents
you make a seamed yard of selves as if on graph paper.
Ed marvels at the enormous scale.
These houses are huge [in fact they're quite small].
Who needs a home this *big* when it's
mean of substance, neither elegant nor interesting?
Except to show how much of you there is; when
there is so little beyond a mower of lawns, a telephoner
of plumbers. For most of his life
he's been ravening
for a solid home.
Well, these homes for the dead
are the same as homes for the living. If this is a home
you can keep it.
To hell with them.

He takes a short cut through a little park near a church
towards Quantock Close.
God! He KNEW it. Why is he surprised?
Dana used to joke — so not a joke then — that there was a stash
sleeping pills in her bedside drawer & 'if you leave me

they'll be my last supper, dear'.
        That's her at the junction of these paths.
She's the grey of death.   He wants to be strong enough
to shun her, but has to race towards her & these two men
beside her (surely her husband & brother). He touches
her cheek — cold as stone. Because it is stone: a statue
of the virgin Mary & two wise men.
        This
                is the pinnacle of the drug which now
shows him the path down from hallucination to
low-key fact.
                He sits on a bench breathing deeply.
He knows he has to *negotiate* this, do it by making nice.
He'll be seeing his unknown uncle soon & the least
he can do is to make nice.   Flowers.
Daffodils are sprouting up in the grass, deep yellow & cream.
If he's quick he can nick some … Yes!
They pull up easily. He has a bunch.

A man in a vest answers the door of number 10.

"Is this the home of Mr Clive Hale by any chance?"

"Nah, he's had to go in a home. *Green Groves Lodge*,
end of street turn right. Yer, jew get them
in the park? Yeah? Better give 'em to I then."
He snatches the bunch & slams the door laughing.

As the cat-lady from the train said,
it has been an overcast day; but now
the sun's out & suburbia is sparkling.
                Here's *Green Groves Lodge*
bathed in light —
a low modern building set in neat parkland.

"Oh, Mr Hale. He loves visitors. You'll find him
in the garden."

To get there Ed must pass through
an enormous lounge area where some kind of party
seems to be going on.
Moira plays *Teenager in Love* on the piano
while Brendan sings *Living Doll* along to it.
Pauline watches
as Gervaise rolls up his trouser-leg to reveal
his scar.
There's precarious waltzing & much laughter.

Sitting under a tree, substantial crutches by his side,
is
Leslie … his dad after death.
Death has drained the colour & force from him leaving
a pale quivering thing: Les to a t, but with a benign-soppy
smile, pure white hair, chalky skin, beige clothes — waving.
Is it Heaven
to be unburdened from your mischief-causing desires?
It's Hell, decides Ed (in the unarticulated thought-language
mentioned earlier).
Clive's voice is nothing like Les' — need I say
it's quivering & thin?
He's heard of Ed but …
"Now this is a LOVELY surprise …" accent a touch of West Country.

"Oooo, can I trouble you for another cuppa Joyce &
dare I ask for a further slice of that *lovely* angel cake?"

The aya has made Ed's sweet tooth even sweeter &
he loves Battenberg cake; but Clive does not
add '& a slice for my long-lost nephew, please Joyce'.

Nurse Joyce asks if Ed would like some tea.

"NO!" he shrieks as the very word spurs thoughts
of more aya. "I mean no thank you, sorry."

Clive talks about the weather & the journey from Bristol
till the tea & cake arrive.

"Oooo you spoil me Joyce. Angel cake from an angel."

The pale pink & yellow cake is about the only cake
you could associate with this man … & when Joyce has gone …

"Bit of soft soap, Edwin. That's what these girls like."

Ten minutes in & Ed has tears in his eyes.
No, he's not moved: these are tears of boredom.
It's the remorseless quest for
the sweet spot of pleasantness & concord. So remorseless
that in Clive's universe nothing can be said
that might excite disagreement or surprise. He talks only
to soothe himself.
If Ed says something
slightly humorous, Clive feels he must suck the remark
dry with more of the same. Or humour — it's only
needed for the pleasantness & sharing — is derived from
popular sitcom references or TV advertisements.
Clive drops
nearly a whole yellow quarter of the cake onto
his pullover, holds it up to the light & sings

"*You'll wonder where the yellow went*
When you brush your teeth with Pepsodent."

He forces himself to laugh; while Ed
wants to cry.
Ed decides to fulfil his flagging
curiosity & bring this to an end.

ED: So how do you come to be here Uncle Clive —
I mean after London.

CLIVE: Now you're asking. Truth be told,
I fell in love with a lady, with my Blanche, the only
gal I've loved & the only gal for me. Blanche, who became
my golden wife. She haled from Gloucester you see &
did not want to move away, so I — now here's a good
pun — came to *Hale* from there myself. We Haled
together.

ED: Very good.

CLIVE: She passed these ten years ago & I moved
down here to the seaside.

ED: Please excuse me saying this Uncle Clive, but
to my eyes you don't seem much like dad
& you're identical twins. You look like him
of course.

CLIVE: Edwin, you are so good
at putting me on the spot. We have the same
kinds of bodies & brains, but you see
we have — do please make allowances for me —
different *souls.*

ED: Can you explain please?

CLIVE: In Gloucester, Blanche & I joined
the *Church of the Golden Thread of Life* —
a breakaway group from the
ROS I CRUC IANS
if you've heard of them. I came to believe
that when we die we go to a place, if we have
been good, in which we are cleansed of our
few remaining stains of sin & then returned
to the upper air as purified souls in new bodies.
Leslie's soul was, maybe, less cleansed
than mine.

ED: *[angrily]* Thank God for that!

CLIVE: Cheeky! *[spluttering laughter]*

ED: Do you know who you were in a previous life?

CLIVE: My name was Kranchiofski & I was a soothsayer
at the court of Frederick the Great of Sicily, Stupor Mundi.

ED: *[with mounting irritation]* And you can remember
being him, if it is a him?

CLIVE: Oh yes, using techniques derived from the
Rosicrucians: you look into a mirror by candlelight—

ED: It doesn't make sense.
How can you be the same person if you DON'T
remember being him in a previous life?
All there is to being me is what I can *remember*
of doing this and that as me. That's *me*.

CLIVE: Ah but you do remember, dear boy.

ED: Always? So, the *evidence* for being the same person
is the *same thing as being* the same person.

CLIVE: Edwin, you have your father's acute penetration.
I'll give you that.
Would you like a wine gum by the way?
Please try to appreciate that the soul
is not the same thing as the thread of conscious
memory of your earthly self — that's a small matter
at least to a fool such as I

[He breaks into the song 'A Fool such as I'.]

Now is that Jim Reeves or Ronnie Hilton?

[A longish period of silence]

ED: I was wondering if you still have
some of the soothsaying skills from your Sicily days.

CLIVE: Oooo yes! & tell you the truth,
this is where you come in.
You will be the bridge dear boy,
an unknowing one methinks
between this kind of world &

a new kind of world that will be with us
in about 50 years or so.
In this new world you will not need to leave
your home

[He luxuriates in this word 'home'.]

to make friends, to meet your future wife, to talk
to your nearest & dearest face-to-face.
We'll be able to do all we used to have to do
outside, inside, in our lounges.
Inside, by ourselves.
We'll do it all with a typewriter with a TV on it
& a little walky-talky with a screen & keys.
We can pick it up & ask it any question & get the answer,
no need for books. That's the beauty of it,
because all knowledge of all kinds, including about
you & other people, is in a kind of cloud that we can
just use.
We can talk to a box & it will play
our favourite tune. No need to go
to concerts.   No need.
All done by ourselves in our lounges.
No need to go out breathing in the germs
of other folks & stepping in dog dirt.
Cosy at home with a screen giving us
knowledge & company.

Ed imagines now a life lead like this in one of
the   *homes*   he'd been
shuddering at under the drug;
then at once recalls the need for a photograph
of him & Clive together & for Clive to sign
the paper.

Joyce is delighted to oblige.
& Clive writes slowly in a beautiful copperplate
hand how 'lovely' their meeting has been.

In the end he has warmed to his uncle.
& in the end he is sure
that if his uncle's predictions for 50 years hence
are true
he would prefer to enter through
the gate of false visions
that aya had afforded him.

Seven: War

"Mr Latimer will be with you shortly, please wait
in the whatdoyoumecallit? —
the morning room or sun lounge."
Her voice is very loud & very rasping — she might easily
be Widow Twanky or one of Cinderella's sisters.
In short, a male thespian most sonorous,
& in this case with Les' walnut skin.
She is eyeing Ed smirkingly.
                    Up to this point

Ed has been buoyant. There's been progress.
Ned has found a live-in job as a dogsbody
in the *Steam Packet* pub beside a stinking
canal-through-mud south of the Centre;
the photo has been developed & left with Miss Grosswald
along with Clive's crafted testimony; she says
all looks good & to get back to her in a week.

Then it was off to the Labour Exchange himself.
Yes! This might be the perfect niche for them both:
Ed's a jack-of-all-works with a strong penchant
for gardens & forests; he's obviously a leader;
he can organise people; there are white-collar elements
about him; yes, he has had experience helping
to run a funfair
(on Richmond Green in '56). Yes, there
will be a fair later in the year. They want him to be paired
with a 'junior' (Ned). In fact, they want a hands-on
administrator to take care of the day-to-day running
of the Blaise Castle Estate in Henbury (N-W Bristol),
focussing on the parkland & play area,
rather than the museum & house.

The 'castle'
is an eighteenth-century folly best known from a distance.
The fair
is the Goram Fair, named after a mythical
local giant,
which happens in summer —
more of this later.

Lester Latimer is the decidedly hands-off administrator
& agent of the Bristol City Council.
They need somebody in place soonest &
Ed is hopeful … But this weird woman!
Her name is Kristin Alsop —
the domestic factotum.

Before a large picture window overlooking the parkland
is a beautiful chess set sat proudly on a table between two chairs
with tall upholstered backs.

"Bet you wouldn't mind A CRACK AT THEM CHESS APPLES!"
says Miss Alsop; & when no reply comes from Ed
she adds:

"Mister Latimer is as fine as pussy fur, but …
he does like A STRAIGHT BACK & SMILE."

It's as if, in the pantomime of her everyday life,
she declaims popular catchphrases from sitcoms & TV ads
loud enough for the nippers as the back
of the theatre to hear.
But she's not —
to Ed at least — a mere eccentric. There is about her
something dangerously ballistic being held back
on a leash, married to a
sly, perhaps pettifogging, ill-intent. Her bodily movements
are also loud & rasping.

"I was going to offer you a cuppa chai but
here comes THE BOUNTY HIMSELF," she says
before departing.

    Lester Latimer
    is dapper, though slow;
    elegant, though shambling;
    solid, though childlike.
    Immediately

Ed is at his ease. Clearly, this man
wishes him well.
He listens, smiling, as Ed describes the challenges
of erecting & dismantling a helter-skelter
in the half-light, the fishy tax arrangements
of some itinerant garden workers, how to separate
marquee-erectors' lunchtimes from handy pubs.
Ned too, from what his dad says, seems 'a perfect fit'.
& when his dad tells Lester how keen & skilled
Ned is at chess the deal cannot help but be done.

"Can I," says Lester, "offer you a sherry? … Now
where's Kristin got to?"

This now is certainly not Kristin, though she could be
in the same panto as her —
peroxided, made-up & trussed-up & stack-heeled,
a burlesque Diana Dors.   Half-close
your eyes & she could be a looker; open them
& there is an agèd figure inside the gaudy shell,
& a domestic tornado to boot.
She is Anita, Lester's wife.

"I've lost my appointments diary. Move
your arse Latty."

She shoves Lester forward on his chair & rifles behind him.

"Pip, Pip! stranger." She does the same to Ed.
She then flings cushions about, using objects
as panic props.

"Err, darling, this is Edwin Hale, who'll be
our new landscape manager — "

"Too busy to meet a soul. Charmed, I'm sure."

Then she's off.
Long silence.

"Well, that was my Lady Wife … But why don't
I introduce you to the other lady of the house,
my daughter Lorraine. She can join us for sherry."
He calls up the stairs:
"Lolly darling! … Can you come down please?"

She keeps to the wall like a cat entering a strange room
looking for the nearest sofa to hide under.
She seems frozen.
                    The thaw is something to behold
                    on seeing Ed.
We see a wide smile lighting up her face & the day.
Living up to her name, she lolls on the settee
between the two men but then demures herself
to fetch drinks.
At first quiet & watchful but gradually dares
a few questions of Ed about London —
the sights, The London Palladium … Is it *really*
so hard to get tickets for *My Fair Lady*?

"It's hard if you can't afford them," says Ed.

At which Lolly laughs fit to burst.
The three chat away merrily for quite a while
with the only shadow for Lester being that

he feels like a gooseberry between these two.
Yes, there's nearly half of Ed's life as the age-
difference between them, but everything
is shiningly obvious. Then,

Anita shoots back in … [pantomime indeed!]

"Lorraine! Are you mad! Martyn will be here
in 15 minutes. These are *not* clothes to wear
to *The Glen*. You look like blinking bloody shop-girl.
Put on the yellow taffeta. Move!"

Lolly freezes again & departs as a mouse.

With them gone, Lester speaks:

"OK, I'll fill you in" — he is pained, in two minds —
"The Glen is only a dancing place at the top of Blackboy Hill,
disused quarry with fairly lights & shrubs, nothing really.
Half of Bristol goes there. They'd let a coalman in.
In fact … er … thing is Ed … "

"Sorry, something up?"

"Tell you the truth, Ed, this Martyn is Lolly's *fiancé*.
From a very well-off family, went to the QEH
(Queen Elizabeth Hospital) school.
Well turned out & all that; but I'm a sceptic about him
& Lolly is too. In fact — "

"MISTER TRUNER IS HERE gentlemen. Early though innee?"

"Thank you Kristin."

& here's Turner himself.
His ironic smile, as ever, is on a rolling boil.
He's as tall as Ed, but a wand beside him.

You might think Uriah Heap: who's come into money,
& emboldened, up for dull nasty mischief.
Routine mischief.

"Hello Less. Keeping well?"

His 'Less' captures Turner in one syllable.
His talk, unless when he needs to impress,
is just below the watermark of actual insult
& far below that of actual wit.
He's too engrossed
in the hulking sight of Ed to feel
the pure animosity coming from him.

"Martyn Turner, meet Edwin Hale — "

"I say, what speciality suiting." He fingers the narrow lapel
of Ed's suit jacket. "Now where did you buy this *amico mio*?"

"In Salisbury."

"Oh, what a droll place to buy
continental fancy dress.
Sows-brie [his attempt at cockney]. Not bought
down at the old Bull & Bush then?"

Lester tries to tell him about Ed's new job &
at this Turner's smile vanishes.

"So, you'll be doing a bit of jolly old gardening then?"

"Not really, no."

"Do you bring your own tools?
Tell you what, I used to watch old, old *thing*
trim the plants around the castle when Lolly
& I were up there *courting*. Used to love

that diagonal belt he wore with his tools on. You know
from shoulder to the opposite hip … Are you following
me Edward?
Baldricks they were called in ancient times.
Do you like a baldrick, Edward?"

"Never heard of them?"

"I know what. You're a modernist & you'll be wearing
a baldrick — "

"No, I shan't."

"So, I'll call you a Modrick. He can be our mascot Less.
& there's an awful lot of him isn't there Less? In fact I could
call you two More & Less."

Only the prospect of the job stops Ed
from flattening him. All he does is to say:

"I was wondering why you're wearing a school blazer
to go dancing."

Martyn hitches up the jacket like an accordion player
adjusting his instrument:
"This jacket is tailor-made from the finest cashmere
in Clifton Village old son.
& THIS is the badge of my old school that I wear
with pride: Queen Elizabeth's Hospital.
Any funny remarks about that & you'll receive more than
a hard look — Modrick — "

Anita bursts in with Lolly in her wake.

"Mar-Mar, darling. You're early you scamp."
She kisses him on the lips. "Sit, sit!"
She settles him in a comfortable chair, & perches on the arm

with her arm over the back.
"Now what have you been up to,
my handsome tallboy?"

Handsome? Hardly.
When Ed doodles he tends to draw a certain male profile,
a cartoon of Turner, as it turns out:
man with a large nose like a triangular proboscis & with
a bump in the middle, bony face, piggy eyes, ears like wings,
hardly a chin at all,
then most distinctive & luxuriated in doodle-wise, hair
in tight waves, tight as a Brillo Pad and with even ridges,
as if flattened back from the forehead by the force of the wind
the nose is facing.

Even when Turner lays his hand
on Lolly's arm
she stiffens,
& when he gives her a peck on the cheek
she shrinks away.

"Plenty of time for that later," Turner declares.
"Not in front of mater & pater eh?"

The three have gone now.

LESTER: You see how things stand, Ed.

ED: Couldn't help it.

LESTER: The missus wants Lolly to marry him.
One, he's filthy rich & two, well she …
likes him.

ED: She certainly is warm towards the berk.

LESTER: You can release us from this … berk.
I know what you think of Lolly.
I'd rather live under Bristol Bridge than be
his father-in-law. You can SEE Lolly's reaction
to him. She confessed to me the other day
that she can't stand him near her …
but she's scared of her mother, you see. You know
she really likes you & I know my daughter.
You have my blessing Ed. I'll smooth your path.
The rest is up to you. Easy stuff.

ED: This is a very special day for me Mr Latimer.

LESTER: Lester, please.

ED: This is the happiest day of my life
Home at last.

LESTER: Eh? Never mind. Let's seal the deal.
I've got a lovely malt.
Kristin!

She cannot reply because she's in the room hiding between
the protruding bookcase & the door.
She slides out of the door, runs down the corridor
& calls back.

"Coming Mister Latimer."

"THERE'S PLENTY FOR YOU LEFT THEN,"
Kristin announces
as she brings in the bottle & a bowl of ice.
Chipper Kristin is full of pep & radiance.

During the happy half-hour Lester explains the accommodation —
a tiny three-room cottage in Blaise Hamlet: "cramped but
handy & picturesque." Then Ed gives a précis
of the saga of the Les legacy & lays out his hope for their future

financial security. Lester decides they should drink to this too, so Ed returns to his son liquid with joy: his very hungry son, who has had no lunch or dinner. The drink has also made Ed hungry, so they get on the scooter & go to look for a food shop that's still open.

A delicatessen — that will do. Pricey, but needs must.

"Hey, look Ned: Pizza pies you can heat up at home."

"Never heard of them dad. Are they big?"

Later, Ed is sitting on the bed reading the *Daily Mirror* & eating his pizza (nothing like he remembers) while Ned sits in the only easy chair in the miniscule sitting room eating his.

"How was it?" says his dad later.

"Well … the top was wizard dad but it was much too chewy for me — I mean the lower deck was. Could hardly get my teeth into it. Not that tasty either. Filling though, I'll give it that."

Ed looks at the wrapping Ned has discarded & sees no sign of the pizza's thick cardboard base. Ned's eaten it & tells him so …

"I couldn't wait dad. I was bloody starving."

"Don't swear son … Finish that brown bread & the fruit … Oh God. Oh my God no!"

"It's not that bad is it dad. Is it fatal?"

"No, I mean … "

This is exactly what Mrs Harpic has predicted,
that tight avian ball of poison gas. 'You will be so hungry
you will eat find yourself eating cardboard' — words
to that effect.

So yet again

Ed descends from Heaven into Hell as he recalls
the rest of her predictions about strife, bloodshed,
& all the kinds of stuff he is gearing up
to avoid. It really does
look that way.

* * *

"Ah Kristin, what can I do for you today?"

"Thing is, Mrs Latimer, I just happened to be returning a cookery tome
to its rightful place on the bookshelf in the morning room or sun lounge
when I could not help but hear Mister Latimer say something
that I think you need to attend to. Thing is I cannot but
be truthful with regard to this FLOATER IN THE WAVES
of my recent memory. Mr Latimer was heard to say
to that Mister Hale that he was all in favour of the Hale fellow
TAKING OVER your daughter Lorraine & poor Martyn
being pushed onto the scrapheap like so much tainted fish.
I can tell you Mrs Latimer IT SHOOK THE TIMBERS
OF MY FRAME OR MIND. What I know is gnawing
a hole in my professional — "

"Shut up, Alsop. Doesn't surprise me in the least.
Here's a ten-bob note to keep your ears open.
Report straight to me anything more along these lines."

Anita is hot to nip buds.
She walks straight into Lester's office without a knock,
controlled, determined, cold, & feeling

she's about to enjoy crushing his plan
& that fairy-looking ponce Hale
like beetles. She can almost hear the crunch.

She begins quietly, ominously, referring to Kristin only
as 'a little bird' (a krekking male corncrake? a honking goose?),
but the smaller the response she gets from her husband
the angrier she grows.

"So, what do you have to say for yourself Latimer!"

"Just that you're wasting your breath.
I will do what's best for my daughter."

"*Our* daughter you mean. What's best for her
is financial security, because the City Council pays you nothing.
She needs money. We all do."

"To hell with that. She detests Turner & so do I.
He makes our flesh creep."

Lester has a gift for immobility, not so much for acting
as for preventing by making himself an obstacle,
for making himself heavy as do some toddlers
when you try to pick them up.

She drops her voice & forces a horrible smile …

"Ah, my rock, my implacable, *strong* rock,
my partner in life — a solid rock."

She tiptoes up to him to tap him on the head:
"Rock for a bloody brain." At which she
bursts into tears & runs away to her room.

The next hour or two are spent phoning 'the girls',
meaning women roughly of her age & similarly

carapaced by make-up & fake-up & who really
do like a drink.   She insists
on a pub crawl around the top of Blackboy Hill,
ending up in Clifton Village. It happens that evening.

She begins, impatient, with the (to her)
'granny-talk', impatient
to get stuck into the filthy jokes & filthy gossip, then
the blurred hysteria of meeting pissed strangers;
falsely believing all the girls will end up in a certain Clifton
Village cellar bar listening to her sad complaints.
        None of them
can keep up with her.
They try to have her drinks mixed with single shots
but she spots this immediately, spitting fury.

At the bitter end she breaks away from the survivors
in Whiteladies' Road saying she's going to find
a cab but finds herself standing then kneeling
in the middle of the closing-time traffic.
                The police bring her
home. In their van she flirts with them happily,
invites them in. She is cautioned when she tugs
at a copper's belt.

"I'll caution *you* sweetie. If you don't gimme
a kish I'll … [*blackout*]."

Miss Alsop has more work to do
early the next day.   She knows the fine house
near the zoo where Turner lives with his parents & knows
he has his own little flat off to the side of it whose bell
she rings & rings   & rings.
                Eventually he appears, punch-drunk
with sleep in a blue silk dressing gown. It's urgent,
she insists, & concerns 'your immediate & PERMANENT future'.
He lies on a *chaise longue* barely able to keep

his eyes open as she goes rounds the houses blowing
soft & LOUD. He gets the message but really
doesn't care that much …

"Well, if the girl is anything like she is now when
we're married, forget it. She's putting out nothing is
Miss Tin Knickers, Miss Immaculate Silence.
The Modrick can have her."
The alteration

in Miss Alsop is out of this world. First,
her anger is a hiss of a nest of snakes;
she comes to the boil, barks in what sounds like
a foreign tongue, & flings out a strong arm
right at Turner's big bumped triangle of a hooter &
twists hard, so hard the pain kills all resistance.
He's now on the floor begging for mercy—
"Fnop, bleaze!"

"You are a GOWNER, you drip, you great streak
of piss. You say you wear your QEH gown with pride,
but you are shitting yourself in the swamp
of your own feebleness. You are a GOWNER
before you are a man!
You must fight.
You must call up ALL the GOWNERS."

At this point I pause to explain the term 'Gowner'.
Since the time of the founder of the school called
Queen Elizabeth's Hospital, the first Queen Liz,
boarders at the school (he was one, though only living a mile
away) have worn a distinctive uniform: a long dark blue or black
floor-length gown overcoat-style, sometimes called a 'bluecoat',
a leather belt, a white clerical starched collar like
a inverted V, grey shorts, knee-length socks, & dress shoes. They
are often seen flapping in the wind around Clifton streets,
or near the school by Cabot tower

like actors in a Buñuel movie
or carrion-eaters.
'Dressing gown boys' — some call them.
Most pupils are glad to see
the back of this fancy dress when they leave school;
but for others (for whom the school is something
between a religion, sports-team, & an absolute condition
for mental thriving) the gown is a transitional object
they just cannot abandon. This lead
to the foundation of a dining club called The Gowners —
demure, rather camp, harmless.

But sometime after the Great War it changed its character,
becoming thuggish & virulently anti-working class. They still
dine in restaurants but instead of leaving a tip they
destroy the place (paying handsomely afterwards … the places
seem to profit by it). The uninformed
think there is a homosexual strain to it all (their 'dresses' etc.),
but the opposite is true. No pretty woman is safe from their attentions
near Gowner-haunted streets after dark,
not with a bunch of them behind her
rosy with claret.
Currently, Turner is the President of the club,
— or 'Big Gown'.

One *slight* twist more on the nose & Alsop knows
that the corner's been turned: his reaction is more anger
than complaint.
She leaves him to it now.

As it was for his soul-mate Anita, the next hour-plus
is given up to phone calls — to the Gowner fraternity
with the instruction to impede (a place-holder, for now)
the 'Modrick' (usage among Gowners spreads), his son,
& more generally the continentals in the more southern
regions of the city. There must be a broad front
in plain sight against all forms of Modrick. Looking

in his shaving mirror he bellows the cry,
the terrible throaty honk that's the call to war on
furniture & fixtures & lower-class obstacles, the mood
music of assault:

'Gowner Gowner Gowner, Amo ODI ODI'

The next stage of Kristin's campaign — I pause again
as the question's spurred: '*Why* a campaign'?
What's in it for her?
Nothing really beyond the satisfaction of causing
failure & pain to somebody she's taken against.
She takes against
not often but violently & when she
does she loves the joyful venom of it all.

Some days pass …

Yes, for the next stage of her campaign
she needs events to percolate.
It needs Ned to get into a rhythm & routine of work
observed at a distance by her.   Poison —
now that is her element.

She notes he needs rat poison to keep down the black
rats who live in the castle folly, that he
keeps a bag of the poison in what she calls
'a cubby or glory hole' near his tool shed;
she notes that loveable old Ernie Craddock's dog
called Bambi (Ernie who has worked on the estate
all his long life & is now like a loved mascot)
often sniffs round this cubby or glory hole.
She poisons the dog, carries it
to the cubby or glory hole
lies the dog beside the bag, which she has
ripped open.
                    Ernie & his allies refuse

to believe it was carelessness (& that's bad enough)
because Ned was once seen to be 'off' with Ernie.
Rumour rushes around the estate & the streets of
Henbury & beyond with its lying boots on: he poisoned
the dog because, well, because he's a poncey London
continental … well his dad is anyway & that's
enough to make him break an old man's heart.

Meanwhile, the Gowners' campaign is advancing.
As most of them are well-off, they can pay handy thugs
to do nasty bits & pieces:
from buttering the round handle of the cottage front door
to removing the Lambretta's wheels & hanging them
from a high branch, to spilling the newcomers' drinks in pubs,
to squaring up to Ed in car parks (always sorely regretted).
They extend

the violence to 'Modricks' further south in the city.
After a dinner (more food
thrown than eaten) in a place on the road
below the bridge near Charlotte Street, some Gowners
flutter up the steps, lead by their pissed brains to the
centre where they destroy scooters with bollards.
One Gowner is caught & his gown torn from him.
The continentals are not effete
& his black-blue-magenta-yellow body,
in its shorts & shiny shoes,
is chased around College Green
by neatly suited men & stray dogs.

Ed reads about this in the *Evening Post,*
reads the quote from 'the Society's President,
Mr M Turner' that this was due to 'just one or two hotheads'
& that the continentals' response was 'obscenely disproportionate'.

Well, it washes over him;
it's bad weather on a different continent.

Closer & worse is the constant insidious campaign against him by
Ernie's self-styled 'little army' of estate workers, contractors,
& the caterers who service it.   It's very easy
to tell the difference between the campaign of what I
shall call 'the Ernies' & that of the Gowners' handy thugs.
The latter is coarse & obvious & childish; the former
sly & insinuating, draining life & point from the working day.

Ned is frequently the target because he does more manual work
& works alongside the Ernies.
He may go to the tool shed & find his best axe
without its head …
"Nooo can't think what happened to that squire.
I'm fair flummoxed" — lifting the flat cap
to scratch the forehead — "can't imagine
whir it could problay be though."

Ned is carrying some bedding plants from here
to there & is tripped up by a couple of painters
sitting on a wall —
"Didn't see you there Nedward. Gotta see the funny side
though eh … eh? Let us help you up." They spill paint
on his hair. Not much, just enough. "Sorry mate!"
          Inevitably   Ned snaps.
Sometimes he goes wild, his lower teeth jutting
like on a bottom-feeding fish.   He lumbers
& they are fleet. His haymakers slice the air with
vicious intent. Once one landed & the man landed
up in the Bristol Royal Infirmary for a week
having his jaw wired up & something done
to his eye.   Of course, this hardly
brings sympathy to the Londoners.

In the office, bins are not emptied, morning tea
spilled on Ed's desk, a jam doughnut is squeezed
over an important document …
& then Ernie, the Ur-Ernie, has a stroke,

a very mild one, but it gives him the excuse to take
to his bed …
"Ee's fuckin' bed-ridden, the poor old soul.
If 'e dies those fuckers'll end up in the fuckin' bridewell."

So yes, as everything is coming to the boil, Turner
decides it's time to join forces
with the 'peasants' (Ernies).
& this is as almost everybody
has forgotten the cause of the dispute.
Almost nobody knows
what the aims of these campaigns are.
While Ed & Lolly have never even been alone together.

But war, like a game in progress,
comes with its own sake.
Who would pause during a football match to ask
why we're doing this & what exactly do we
need to bring about. It's wonderfully free of
the examined life.

The Ernies have no spokesman — which is how Turner likes it.
He meets & treats & flatters some of them & proposes a
meeting with Lester Latimer — which happens in about
two weeks' time in the morning room or sun lounge.

TURNER: Our demands are simple Lester — if I can still address you this way.

LESTER: Yes of course Martyn, & it's very nice to see you all here on this lovely morning.

TURNER: We demand that Hale father & Hale son
be dismissed forthwith & that the father donates, let's say,
£300 to poor Ernie Craddock to compensate him for the loss
of his dog & for the stress subsequent leading to his
loss or slight loss of the use of his left hand & his bedridden
state.

LESTER: But what has the business of the dog got to do with you Martyn? Won't you bring yourself to admit that you are not remotely exercised about this but rather piqued at my daughter's preferring Edwin Hale to you.

TURNER: *[angrily]* You miss the point. The point is a practical & public one. The Gowners have always supported worthy local causes. We give to charity. We see now certain local peas … local workers struggling — good Bristol men — being victimised & having to cope with this spiv interloper.

LESTER: Why do you talk such nonsense Martyn? You don't believe a word you're saying. Hale is an excellent worker. Plans for the Goram fair are being advanced wonderfully & this *despite* the impedances you and your friends & of course Ernie's supporters put in his way. He is staying. For one thing, who would we find to take his place at this late stage? The fair would suffer.

ERNIE-ONE: Trev Markesbury could do it boss.

ERNIE-TWO: Pete Griffin. He taught the turd all 'e knows.

ERNIE-THREE: Trish de Burgh could do it an all. I know she's a tart but she's more like a bloke really.

ERNIE-FOUR: We just don't like him boss. Cockneys don't belong yer.

TURNER: Do you not realise that this business has gone beyond its cause. The Hales have lifted a stone … they've shone a light on … they've rubbed our noses in —

ERNIE-ONE: Fer fuck's sake Mart.

TURNER: They have revealed a form of cultural warfare on-going here that will have its own momentum so long as this irritant remains. You could stop this if you acted & nipped it in the bud.

ERNIE-THREE: Bit more than a bud Mart mate.

LESTER: I don't want to act, I mean, I am not minded
to act in this direction. Good day gentlemen. Please find
your own way out.

When they had gone Lester comforts himself that
he has stood firm … well, he has stood still.
But he wants to lie,
to sleep.
He's 62 only, but would love a gently unconscious death
lying out on his long leather sofa in this room
in the summer sun —
escaping from the world
in which lives his termagant wife
& these nasty, stupid, stupid people.

Eight: Teds

"Yes, if you like."
"Whatever you wish."
"I suppose so."

My God, this girl plays her cards close to her chest,
Ed thinks.
Who is she when she's alone?
What, does she enjoy, want —
apart from tickets to *My Fair Lady*?

At last, this is their 'first date'
& they are walking down the steep pavement of Park Street,
past the Music Shop, *en route* to the cinema for 1.30.
He would have liked them to lunch in the Wimpy Bar,
just here, but this plan was vetoed by her mother —
who also seems to have vetoed her.
It seems, though,
a hot drink is allowed so they double back
& cross over to the Kardomah. Why
does he persevere?
He likes her (more than that) &
his *I Ching* throws have been in a single direction:
Wooing a young girl; Marriage; Family; Peace;
Standstill leading to joy; Termination
of the life of 'a traveller'. There is also the warning
that there will be difficulties in the beginning, or
'Birth Pangs'
as the oracle puts it. He knows that already.

But right now
he wonders if the silence & seeming indifference
might not be preferable to what comes next …

His frothy coffee is surprisingly strong. This
& the brown sugar he's piled in leads him to say this:

"Sorry to say this Lolly, but
you do sometimes give the impression that your life
can be a bit of a burden to you sometimes."

Out it spills … Introspection is clearly her hobby
& clearly she's been 'seeing' somebody to fuel it.
She calmly admits to low self-esteem, 'hesitancy
before life's choices,' a 'yearning for fulfilment
in my proper metier', & a 'desperate need to find something
to commit myself to'. She lacks confidence & knows
she does, in short.

"Sorry to hear that Lolly; but do you think maybe   uh
your   uh   *mother* could be holding you back   somehow?"

She presents him with an almost-pitying smile then
gives smoothly three reasons why this is
'a naïve misreading of the situation'.

She does, though, enjoy the film.
She squeezes his hand in excitement when Hercules
(played by Steve Reeves, as ever), with his bare inverted triangle
of a torso, flattens something or other by
chucking a cardboard rock at it in the Californian sunshine
of ancient Greece.
Cobalt sea & sky & gold of sand & fixtures & oiled poses.
Then he squeezes her forearm in something like excitement
when Steve lifts his face skywards & says:

"I am getting sick of doing these labours for the GADS."

The gads explain that he's a bit of a gad himself,
but never mind: it touches Ed's disposition.
Who is making him go through all this stuff:

Ioanna, Dana, the crazy games & silly old Clive
& now Ernies & Gowners. Whose idea was it?

In these two moments of touch did
the purple & pink serpent of the erotic poke its head
between the fissure of their joint consciousness?
Not exactly no; but Hercules'
words are how it is with Ed.

In fact, there *is* something Herculean about Ed,
& something of the victim too. He's too big for the Ernies,
& the Gowners are backing off — for now.
There have been advances too, as we shall see.
But his mind cannot get away from this tar-baby thought.
This girl says she has life problems, he thinks to himself, while
it says to me:
'Here's your favourite pudding then, just watch out
for the shattered razor blades I've mixed in with it
just to make things interesting for us'.

The outright war with Turner & his merry men
will come & he's ready for it, a readiness
aided by their now having money.
Yes, Les' money materialised quickly —
though much depleted by legal fees.
There is enough to buy a little house; but
why settle now while all this strife is brewing?
Instead, they are renting a maisonette
about a mile from the estate.
It's the sanctuary Ned deserves after long days
of bearing the brunt of the Ernies' bile.

Ned is changing.
He's losing weight with the sweated labour,
making his face gain definition:
cheek-bones seem to appear overnight like mushrooms.
He's quicker in body & mind now, so his wild haymakers

& spat-out threats cause fewer guffaws.   Of course,
he loves all they have now that they never had before:
a fridge, TV, telephone, record player, running hot water.
He delights in shows like *Oh Boy* & *Drumbeat,*
the latter of which inspires him to train his hair
into the style of Adam Faith's, having had a long period
under the regimen of the Jess Conrad barnet. Ned's blondeness
helps this along. With the flattened & twisted blonde
coiffure above his new cheekbones he's quite
a plausible Adam, albeit a giant one … The result?
the girls show an interest & so does he.

He loves how in Bristolian 'girl' is pronounced 'grill'.
In fact, they both call them grills now, with a group
of young women of radically mixed attractiveness
being a 'mixed grill'.

It's his father who has to keep
the show on the road, especially now Lester
has withdrawn from the front line. Yes, Lester's rock-like
but waves & weather wear rocks away.
Inside he seems to waver.
As for Ed himself, he doesn't sleep.
All through the night his consciousness never retires:
it flickers like sunlight on the black wavelets
of his concerns, till he wakes armoured for the day,
later to collapse.

He collapses now, drops off during the film's
climax in which Hercules completes his final task
& bellows at the gads. He wakes with his head
on her shoulder, awakes
to people squeezing past him &
God Save the Queen.
                              She allowed his head
to stay put because she likes it there & when
their eyes meet they know — let's put it this way —

that these birth pangs will produce
the rosy-cheeked infant of their love.
Their silent walk
to the foyer is sweet,
but the hot daylight freezes her again.
No matter —
much has been achieved by accident.
They're not back at the starting block.
She's happy to catch a bus home & leave him
to mooch around town after a parting
which is low key & full of meaning.

A free Saturday afternoon
in the sun.
Hercules is back as he stands at the dolphin-haunted
foot of Neptune on the dock-end of The Centre, commanding
the water: subject to a thirst to do big deeds, while feeling
the constraint from above. An adventure on water is what
he desires — to which the trident points perhaps?
It points to:

Tibbs' Avon Boat Adventures
Today:
Fry's Chocolate Factory

Perfect.
Already a couple aboard;
but no sign of Mister Tibbs till he emerges
as if from the water itself just behind the stern,
smiling & generally being nice.
There is not exactly niceness so much as splendour
in the couple sitting together at the prow;
but surely not a couple. Has to be

father & daughter. Splendour?
Of the Teddy 'Boy'.

No 'boy' this — old man rather,
built like a barrel, the kind of body
that has spent a lifetime on building sites.
Ed, as we know, is statuesque & bulky,
but this character is probably harder
& a better fighter.
The long sides of his grey hair are Brylcreemed up
as a declaration of violent intent. No hair
to speak of on top, but the sides are long enough
to be winged like chariot sides, to converge
on the crown and curve down into a tassel-like
fringe in homage to Gene Vincent as if to say:
'This is what I'll do to yr fuckin' limbs
if you gives me any cheek'.
                                    All of which
is immediately given the lie by the open
welcoming smile he gives Ed …

"Alright cock?"

Ed almost misses this greeting because he's fixed
on the daughter …

Male Teds have a costume: drape coat, drainpipe trousers,
luminous socks, beetle-crusher shoes, bootlace tie (all
wonderfully in place on the dad). But the Teddy Girl
is nothing more than a commercial invention, like Fathers' Day.
In TV pop shows she is safe & vague.
Not this, oh not this, not this with a vengeance:
pink leather jacket, much zipped; skin-tight black
jeans that end halfway down the calves; ankle bracelet;
high heels; black t-shirt with a white neckerchief;
Cleopatra-style eye-liner most emphatic;
a kind of French roll that adds 7 inches to her height.

'There's nothing of a Teddy here.
All you've described is a Tearaway Tart'.
You might alliterate &
you would be wrong.
It is the girl herself, her choosing to dress so, despite
a nature with nothing of tearaway or tart.

She is in constant motion & even when still there's a
slight quivering, like a fish that's just been landed
onto the boat; except she is actually a water sprite.
She often shares little inaudible jokes with her dad, carries
a handbag-style radio. In fact, she speaks to Ed,
about the playing radio …

"This bother you?"

"Not at all. I like the sax as a matter of fact."
A Little Richard number is playing with a jazzy tenor solo.
Their words are enough to establish a rapport as two
families take up their positions down the other end
with Tibbs.

"Down from London then?" (Dad)

"Yeah. Been working up on the Blaise Estate."

[PAUSE]

"I knows about you."

Dad's been reading the *Evening Post* & knows all about
Ed versus the Ernies, about how his presence has stoked
the Gowner-Continental conflict.

"One of our Patsy's mates was attacked by a Gowner."

"I'm Patsy, by the way, & the 'mate' was a girl."

From what they then go on to say, Gowners are
a natural phenomenon like a pestilence for the dad.
But for Patsy,
the are too-thriving agents to be hated & harmed
one-by-one.   It seems the main reason
Teds & Gowners are not in open war is that the former
are strong south of the city & the Gowners strong
around Clifton Downs & some points north.

The dad is outspoken. As the engine fires up & a whiff
of petrol wafts towards them he seems to be mulling over
the Gowner-Teds situation, but it's Ed who's
being mulled:

"Bit big to be a continental ain't you?"

"Yes."

"& you're a bit old to be a Ted, dad."

"But I'm a King darlin."

In fact, he is. So much becomes clear to Ed.
He knows much in detail about the distribution
of Ted forces throughout the city, while using phrases
like 'I told 'em to do it. Need to get up there
& sort 'em out'.

"You can help can't you dad? *We* can."

The boat chugs along the docks & out into
sweet green countryside in a Bath direction.
Tibbs half-heartedly begins a commentary to which
dad responds: "Put a sock in it Gar*ay*!"

Suddenly a hand is thrust towards Ed …
"Georgios Eviades. Pleased to meet you."

My God, he's a bubble. George has taken his drape off
now & is sitting serenely with it across his knees becoming
the form of these low-slung
Greek seniors who congregate towards
sundown at café tables by the sea, telling their
beads & keys, while the womenfolk
keep the home fires bubbling.
There's a sudden smokiness
about — no, not smoke, *cocoa*. The water
becomes brown till they could be sailing
in a bedtime drink beside the high Victorian
brick-face of Fry's factory. Deliciously smelling
brown dust is occasionally
emitted. What a glory then: the marriage of chocolate
& the fine greenery & low hills, weird background
to their Ted talk.
As Tibbs turns the boat back to the docks
George is clear & decisive:

"Tell ee what I'll do Ed. You come down to Southville next week
& I'll take you up Hartcliffe & Knowle West on the bike.
Call in to a few boozers, get some of the hardest
bastards alongside. They all got bikes so they can
shoot up & say how-do to a few fuckin' Gowners."

"That's great George."

"Yer, how you fixed at the moment?
I mean for gelt?"

"Right now, we're doing well."

"Good. Our Patsy needs a job.
You take her on as a live-in cook, cleaner
& general fackotum & she'll get all the northern
forces lined up.
One look at she dolled up and they'll be
on the floor frothin' at the fuckin' mouth."

"Daaaad."

Ed hears himself saying: "I think we could squeeze her
into the box room," then muttering something about
buying a camp bed while all the time thinking
'This is madness! I've learned nothing — inviting
BUBBLES into my house … '
But agree he does;
he does so because of Patsy. Much could be said
as to why & much more should be kept unsaid.
Yes —
he is 'frothing at the mouth' in his pious, dignified manner
but sweating with guilt at doing so. With guilt & confusion …
Ned … or rather the Giant Adam Faith whose erotic imp
is beginning to sit up & take notice. Patsy & Ned together
in the flat — sharing a bathroom!

Patsy herself is delighted, does a little dance
& in a high pure voice sings (all sailors' eyes upon her)
a current hit, a snippet of whose chorus is

Cha-Cha Chicken & a pizza pie —
Go ape man.

None of the adults on the boat fail to record this
as reference to Ed's continental tonsure
& rig-out.

Ed proudly flourishes his phone number as the three of
them part on the docks, making the arrangement for Ed
to come down to Southville on Monday to meet George —
eleven am outside the *Hen & Chicken* pub in North Street.
His thoughts are fully on Patsy, not on the coming war or 'war'.
To think about war is to be Hercules Chained & he is
being chuted down a white-water stream to unchaining.

Standing back from himself & weighing the black chain
in his hands he takes the view:

he's left it to Teds — to Teds! — to do what he
& other 'contis', as Teds call them, should be doing himself.
Does he want Teds — a *Greek* Ted who'll kill his failing sleep —
to be a housemate. He has gone along with it
because of the gorgeous water-sprite
now half-skipping beside her dad as they cross The Centre
to where his magenta Norton 1000cc is parked.
                                        But
can't he go along with his heart for once in his life?
Lolly is lovely, but a mother-haunted freezer;
whereas Patsy is a perfect *female.* Love?
Sometimes it's got to make way for life.

Yes, he's confused enough. So those twin resolvers
of this mental state — the Chinese oracle & his mother Lady Vera —
must be called upon.

Ned — making an *Airfix* model of a Lancaster bomber
at the kitchen table — knows at once his dad's state of mind
when he gets back, when he goes straight into the bedroom
from which coins chink. ('The I chink' Ned calls it.)
When he emerges half an hour later his dad's face is a mixture
of disappointment & relief.   Ed doesn't think

he's ever had a more consistent set of readings:
consistently contradicting in the same way —
strife & evil plus nirvana-like peace & triumph —
with every hexagram carrying both. No,
he has no 'erotic future' with Patsy at all;
but in his future with her there will be some
transcendent outcome. After a terrible battle
they run off together to join
a celibate religious order?

"Don't tell me dahrling. I know all.
You poor, poor creature. Those DREADful
Gown-Boys or Gownies or whatever they are —

disgrace to the upper middle-class *esprit*.
I know it all, precious fox."   Of course,

Vera would never read *The Evening Post*, but
she happened to sit next to its owner at dinner
& they did get talking about 'cultural tensions'
in the city & 'the debasement of the public-school ethos'.

"Listen dahrling. I have, if not the solution,
at least an interesting nudge towards a hint
of mitigation.   No, it's not one of
my gals this time. It's an ex of mine.
I'm not really in touch with him but by George
is he in touch with me.   Terribly seedy
& boffiny these days but goodness you should
have seen him just down from Trinity Cambridge
in the summer of '35.

Dr Vincent Hogan works in the Department
of Engineering at Bristol University & has severe animus
against the Gowners.
He has been ruminating on practical methods to
discourage the marauding gents ad lib.

Get on the blower to the Varsity dahrling.
You'll track him down by the smoke signals
he sends up, like a red-
Indian *encampment*, poor blossom."

As it turns out, they speak that very evening.
Ed gives his phone number to everybody & of course
to his mum, who passes it on to Vince when he calls
her to ask what she's doing 'for Saturday night'.
Father & son jump out of their skin when the phone rings
& Ed answers sounding like a terrified choirboy "S-speaking.
H-Hale residence. Who is there on the line *please*?"
Vince suggests coming into the lab the next day,

despite its being Sunday … "chew the fat … stoke up
the furnaces of creativity & resentment."

Ed finds him sitting on a high stool manipulating
something that looks like a wired-up garlic press,
a cigarette dangling from his lips, a lick of thick
white hair lolling over his forehead — stained cigarette
brown. He is fleshy & kindly & certainly unsavoury.
He barely registers Ed & goes on twiddling.

"Pesky thing! No, I tell you what, Edwin. I used to
have a flat in Cotham village next to *Les grenouilles*,
lovely little place.
The Gowners took it over & didn't just demolish it,
they demolished the faith in human nature
of all humans there or even nearby. The things
I saw in the street outside at 2 in the morning."

Note in passing that at these 'dinners'
& at all events that are officially 'Gowner Galas',
as they call them, the uniform must
be worn. Anybody who does not wear the full
regalia is debagged & his genitals smeared with jam.
Anybody who does not walk straight-backed & proud
in public in his gown when he should
is the worst form of coward.
Given all this

Vince has decided to make the gown itself his focus —
its long flowing vulnerability. If you attack the gown
you get the Gowner.
"Come," he says & they go down some corridors
to his office.
"I don't have these prototypes out in public spaces;
but smoking's better there."
It is a window-less room with an atmosphere
like a tunnel a split second after the train has departed.

He goes into a cupboard & removes two things:
a strip of thick dark material on a metal frame
& what looks like a stainless steel praying mantis
containing three differently coloured buttons
above a belly-like fuselage.   "Fact is

after the night of *Les grenouilles* I set myself the task
of inventing something that the Everyday Weak-kneed
Pedestrian, or 'EWP', could use against these creatures.
Imagine, they are leaving a venue
after a wood-splitting luncheon,
arms over one another's shoulders,
threatening violence to local tradesmen & worse:
to office girls …
Up behind them comes an 'EWP' with one of these efforts.
He or she aims this at the hem of gown &
presses the green button … "

He points the 'head' end towards the cloth, there's
wet squirt & an overpowering smell of petrol.

"Then, very quickly, he will press the red button.
But, first stand back. Its range is over three feet."

A snake's tongue of flame jets out & the cloth flares up.

"Then you press the blue button, IF you are so inclined,
at your convenience."

Another jet, this time of white foam, smothers the flame
so that a well-charred half remains.

"The decision is yours. If he is behaving like an egregious
bastard, burn him up. Leave the blue button alone. He'll
probably be able to get the gown off anyway. But, who cares?
If he is just performing their standard shit then burn the
gown up to his silly shorts deftly applying Mister Blue.

See if
they can see the funny side."

Vince goes on to explain that he's found a small local
engineering company
to manufacture the praying mantises, but
for an astronomical sum of money.
"I'm not
a rich man, but my mother's recently passed away leaving me
everything.
But what do I have to spend it on? Never settled down.
Never managed it after your mother."

"Same here mate," Ed feels like saying.

"Actually, I've got two of these made up — final year
research projects — I'll give them to you to try
& if they work, as they say, 'in the field' I'll get
forty made up; the more the cheaper per unit."

"That's wonderful, Vince. I'm speechless.
But do you mind if I step outside for a bit?
Catch my breath."

"Let's both step outside.
Let's go back to the main lab. I've got
something to show you."

Well, Ed has been shown enough for one day
& he is only pondering right now how
he can carry two of these things on the scooter.

"We use this for practical classes."

In the corner of the lab there is a screen
& film projector.

"Sit! It's only 8 mil, but adequate.
Let me explain.
Last year, as part of the end-of-exams celebrations,
all members of staff were invited to make a short film
to show just before the party.
Mine was well received, very well received indeed,
Fag?
I'm going to show it to you because
it deserves to be less widely known"

Vince laughs hard at his own joke, causing
a lung-vomiting cough that leaves him still quivering
as he threads the film into the projector. As he is doing
this, between off-cuts of the main cough,
he says he forgot to tell Ed that their brief was to
predict the distant future of their field of engineering.
"They thought I was having a laugh,
but — basically — I was deadly serious."

Vince is a black dot approaching the camera on Clifton Downs.
Suddenly he shoots forward in three steps till he is staring
down the lens within a couple of seconds, a technique
he's borrowed from Spike Milligan.

"What," he begins, "sets the limit on human progress?"
He shrugs himself away from the camera &
strides stage left a la Alan Wicker …
"It is the human mind itself, *that's* what.
We have wonderful scientists, though scientists themselves
are a miniscule proportion of the population.
But most humans have utterly *pathetic* cognitive capacities.
We are limited severely
in *memory* … "

A clip of a schoolboy chewing his pencil as he gazes up
to the ceiling.

"We are hopelessly *poor & slow at reasoning*."

A clip of a chess game between somebody dressed
as a chimp & somebody in subfusc costume. The chimp
is knocking over the other's King in a gesture of mate.

"And we are driven by *emotion*
when we should be cool & dispassionate."

Clip of a policeman who has just caught a sexy young
woman committing a traffic violation.
She is trying to persuade him to let her off
with much eye-lid fluttering. He gazes into her eyes
& is dazed as only Oliver Hardy can be; he rips up
the ticket in a gesture reminiscent of Oliver
twiddling up his little tie into his face.

Voiceover:
"What will the Future do about this?"

Clip of Vince standing at the approach-road
to the Clifton Suspension Bridge, legs
wide apart, hands on hips
dressed in academic gear.

"We recruit the digital computer — the
coming fact — *to do memory & thinking for us*,
so we can put our feet up on the handlebars
& rally down hill … "

Clip of boy doing just this.

Then images of room-sized computers in Manchester
University & in the US military intercut with
images of real & schematic human brains.

"Scientists know that the brain is nothing more
than a super-computer.
In the future
our computers will get smaller & faster & cheaper
so that one day even the homeless will be
carrying one about.
People won't need a good memory because
the world's knowledge will be in their pocket."

Clip of a globe being stuffed in what could pass for
a large pocket (in fact a saddlebag).

"The beauty of it will be that you can be
as stupid as you like, but
computing brilliance will carry you through."

Clip of somebody dressed as a country bumpkin
with joke-shop teeth & straw in his hair
typing on a keyboard.

"You key in the elements of your problem
& the computer will output your answer."

Clip of the printout saying in bold
'Divorce your wife & move to Bridgewater
with the dogs'.

"One of the enormous plusses of all this
is that the Turing machine can deliver judgements
without bias or shame or anxiety, without self-consciousness.
Given this, a person will receive negative judgements
without animosity."

Clip of two men sitting either side of a desk,
one in a business suit & tie, one in dungarees & a muffler.
Suit — "I'm sorry to tell you Mr Bloggs that

you are not eligible for the dole. I recommend
that you become a beggar for a living."
The dungaree man bursts into tears, collects himself
then punches the suit.
Next clip …
The dungaree man presses a key before a screen
and the words 'NO, REFUSED, Sorry'!
pops up.
He looks at the screen, shrugs ruefully
& picks up what could be a begging bowl.

We return to Vince in his smoke-filled bunker
addressing the camera as himself.

"But there will be drawbacks to this future power.
Who's power & for what?
Those not versed in the intricacies of technology
as well as the can't-be-botherds
will find themselves reduced to data points,
to symbol strings that are 'computed over',
while the real power rests with the technocrats
& their ringmasters in politics & big business.

The former will have the illusion of great power —
the world at their fingertips from all human history
art & music to their local *Fine Fair* supermarket,
the little computer in their pocket — their slave.
But *they* are the slaves for this simple reason.

They are the manipulandees … Hey is that a word Josh … ?"

Vince shouts over the soundtrack "Whoops!
More haste less speed."

"They have no say in the information that is fed to them
because they no longer have to go looking for it.
Most gravely, their votes can be manipulated for this reason.

& even if they know they are being manipulated,
what can they do about it?
To this you may say … "

Clip of a Billingsgate costermonger, cap
at a jaunty angle, little red & white-spotted kerchief
saying in the broadest of cockney …

"NEVER MIND EH?"

"Or you may say … "

Clip of a roomful of men and women
all wearing Alan Turing masks saying
DO MIND EH!

The film ends & Ed sits dumfounded.
He half understands what that was all about.
But, the half of him that does not,
& that sees this as no more than
a Rag-week entertainment,
has his tongue so tied that
he can only mumble: "Thanks …
for everything."

Nine: Neil & Ewan

Ed is away; Ned holds the fort.
He holds it by playing his favourite records
whenever he wants to as loud as he likes:
Poor Me and *What Do You Want?* feature heavily;
his Adam Faith course set.
He holds it
by meeting up with a couple of young guys
he's just palled up with — they'd come to do a bit
of light tree-
surgery on the estate — called Neil & Ewan (a lot
more of them soon) & playing around the shop-windows
of the nearest High Street. Soon
the game will light up television but for now it's
a folk passion — the 'split leap'.
You stand before the plane-glass corner of a shop window;
the corner splits your body (nose-halved) & you raise
the leg & arm street-side. Note well
that there is a mirroring of this body-half in the window —
so it appears as if perfectly symmetrical you
are leaping miraculously in the air,
or suspended. You can be an expanding & contracting
crazy star-fish or suspended
like a modern reworking of Leonardo.

Why is Ed away? The trip to Southville to see Georgios Eviades
expanded in an unpredictable way. He climbs
aboard the Norton & they head down to Hartcliffe, a modern estate
of council housing south of the city abutting
rural Somerset with its cider pubs. A nest of hard-nuts.
The feeling's one of emptiness of a tree-free un-suburban kind.
Grey, pebbledash houses with muddy gardens — a battery farm.
Pubs are the only hubs.

First they try a sprawling ranch of a pub
called *The Burning Ship* & head straight for the snooker room.
Yes, these could well be off-duty Teds —
given the hair and air of caught violence,
the steel combs doubling as daggers
in the top pockets, the fags behind the ears, the constant
re-pompadouring after a lock-lapse. They all

recognise George & do the Ted equivalent of standing to attention:
(legs very wide apart, arms behind backs,
quizzical James-Dean-like frown, furtive settling of
the balls in the jeans.

"Old Mark Binding about?" says George.

"Ooo, he's under petticoat government right now … "
& some other things Ed fails to catch because of the accents.
What does it mean?
George takes a small swarthy guy to one side & seems
to explain the situation about Ed which leads to him
being less ignored & less sniggered at. Nothing
seems to be doing, so George has a game with them,
enabling Ed to become an anthropologist
of Ted culture, south Bristol, late '50s. He
has the required curiosity.

Why
do the natives say "Prick the banDIT!" when
they pot a ball or see their mate pot one?
What
is the relationship between
emitting a loud fart & emitting the phrase
'Suck 'e!!!!'?
Why
do clear failures evoke cries of 'Fuckin' Emos!'
(to rhyme: 'He knows'),
while

"Emos!" is also, when shouted in unison
and with two syllables on 'os', a term of greeting or approbation?
Is
there a reference to contraception in their oft-sung song
'How can you teeeellll a Joey
J   O   E   Y   Joey'?
Why
are so many of them bandy legged?
Is
it an affectation?

They call George 'Skip' and often spit beer at
one another through their teeth.   These men
do not have the makings of an army.
Much the same story in the pubs of Knowle West.
They then try
the wood-yard at the bottom of Hartcliffe Way.
        Only seeing George from the back, initially,
the foreman is about to tell him to clear off,
but when he sees who it is he's deferential.

"Micky Binding? Can help you there George.
Made the mistake of having that head-banger
in the gang last Easter. Never again.
Tell you what I heard in *The Happy Landings* though:
he shagging some tart out in Portishead for the foreseeable.
Try *The Nereïd Arms* by the new pool. And tell the fucker
he owes me five quid."

Ed enjoys the exhilarating ride fast along the Avon Gorge
under the Suspension Bridge then down the estuary
to Portishead. Lòw key industrial, none of the Severn Beach
resort-pretence; but it too has a beach
that's not a beach.   There's a call-box near it
from which he calls Ned who is luckily at home (he's
invited Neil & Ewan back for a mug of *Camp* & a bun).
He seems to be echoing Shirley Temple …

"Hello there. My name's Ned Hale. *What's yours?*"

"My name's your father … Look I'll be late home tonight."
He explains why.

They do find Micky Binding. Maybe it's the first flush
of old-love, but he's dressed in all his Ted finery, and so
is his 'tart' (not one at all) called Betty. The two of them
together, plus Betty's young kids, all dressed Ted —
like a Pearly Wedding in the East End, thinks Ed.
Mick, George & Ed share a table, when they turn
towards the others it could be a Yalta photo-shoot.
Upshot is that Mick gives Ed numbers to call if
Turner 'comes the cunt'. Well, that's progress. But this

isn't: the bike won't start. They're stuck there for a while.

"Hello there! … My name's … "

"Quiet you twerp! … " His dad explains that they'll be staying
at least tonight at George's cousin Ella's in Portishead.

That evening Ed sits on a bench on the front looking out
at the factory lights of Wales watching Micky, Betty, the kids
& a few more jiving with a kind of reverence
to Eve Boswell's *Pickin' a Chicken*
playing on three little transistors.
Silhouetted, his drape & her dirndl skirt bodying forth
symbolising nothing.
Some minds may call up *The Seventh Seal*.
Not Ed's, despite his love of 'continental films'.
But his heart is magnanimous enough to call up
something brave & innocent that he wants
to defend.

When the next day he calls Ned to tell him that the
mechanic says it could take two days the line is dead.

This is because a handy thug acting on Turner's instructions
has cut the telephone cable.   This is how
it came about.

Initially, Neil & Ewan decided to ally themselves
with Ed for reasons of clothes.
There was no principle leading them to him
(as do the Gowners, they referred to the Ernies
as 'peasants'). They liked Ed's sartorial style
& his scooter; all that was enough initially.

Ned was surprised when the two of them turned up
for work on the first day in their best clothes,
as if they were a kind of skin, only changing into
dungarees at the last moment.   Ned
has never seen
                    two more fastidious men.
They wear
that rare thing — Levi blue jeans, in a condition
that for women's clothing you would call 'bandbox fresh'.
They wear the hens-teeth item — shirts with button-down
collars, & striped shirtings more generally.
They fail to despise M&S and C&A & wear immaculate
short-sleeved pullovers from them in pastel shades,
cashmere more often than not.   On their feet
are suede Hush Puppies in a colour like cow-shit.
They are small with straight backs.
Their hair?
You might say they wear Perry Comos.

Beyond the sartorial, however, they struggle
with their chosen genre. They know
modern jazz is *de rigueur* but are uncertain
as to what it is.   On solid ground
they are with The Modern Jazz Quartet,
but they don't actually like it tinkling softly away.
Buddy Greco ('hup! hup!') has a kind of 'modern-ness'
they can relate & listen to. & on the home front

there is *something* modern about Denis Lotis
(unlike Frankie Vaughan).   Here is a case, then,
of reach exceeding grasp &, my God,
their reach can be almost terrifying.
They are ravening for fame or notoriety, money,
& to have the 'best' women (while not actually
bothering much
about free-range women
at the present time).
Their ambition & their, let's-call-it, ruthlessness
glue them together & they decide that Ed
is their route to these & his son the conduit.

While they look similar, they are quite different.
Neil is hard & fairly magnanimous; Ewan
soft & fairly vicious. That Neil is fearless can be seen
in how he rushes up trees & sways in their branches
like a heavy squirrel (while Ewan tidies up what descends
& generally shouts things out). It's in evidence too
in the way Neil fights when called upon to fight:
he'll take on anybody, but he lacks the killer's touch.
Ewan seeks the killer domain, but lacks
the wherewithal. He is much younger than
his friend & has yet to shave. Close up
his skin has the light down of a peach
or an old lady.   Ned

has always been easy to befriend. They would
pretend to have forgotten their lunch boxes &
he would make them toasted cheese in the maisonette
in scheduled breaks or heavy rain. Sometimes they would
have a game of darts, letting Ned win.   The dartboard
is Ned's pride & joy, especially now it's surrounded by
a white-painted tyre to protects the paintwork of the door.
            It was Ewan's plan, but it is for Neil
boldly to get the ball rolling. Ed's being stuck in Portishead
for a couple of days or more is the perfect opportunity.

"Tell you what," begins Neil, "I was thinking that as
your dad's away and that it gives you a really good opening
to do something of your own — though with our help
like — to get at Turner & the Gowners … "

One of the plusses of these two for Ned is that
he can actually understand what they are saying.
They speak clearly, clearly for Bristolians that is,
who tend to mumbling & slurring.
The clarity of articulation is something
they hit upon after seeing a TV documentary about
'The Youth of Today'.
Interviewed in a coffee-bar dive, the kind of people
they aspire to be had crisp (over-crisp) articulation
(probably drama students); & this wheeze stayed with them.
It comes easily to Ewan, more easily because he
is almost middle class — with an over-protective
dotting mother in fact.

"I know where Turner lives, see, & where he parks
his lovely little Morgan sports-car that was A Present
From Daddy [maximum articulation here]. We thought
we'd leave something surprising on the motor,
shake him up a bit like."

"What?"

"Aaaah. That can be a surprise for you an all.
You'll like it. Guarantee mate."

Ned is thinking. He wants to be in league with these
two in some way & there is nothing he'd like more
than to do something like this off his own bat — or
at least give it the nod. His dad always says
he lacks initiative. This reflection spurs a major
blunder. He decides to show them the 'mantises,'
as I shall continue to call them.

He doesn't activate them.
He just shows them which button does what.
Ewan just can't contain himself.

"Cor Ned. We'll make good use of these — "

"But — "

"Don't worry," says Neil, "we've handled this
kind of thing before. Part of our weed-control
course at the horticultural college." A creative lie.

"Well — " Ned.

"Give 'em yer." Neil grabs them. "Fact we'd
better get back now,
tidy up the spinney by the castle field. Better say
cheery-bye for now."

Ned knows this is wrong. He's at a loss,
wishing hard he could phone his dad. If only
he'd call now. But is it wise to tell him?
Is it too late?

The next day Neil tells him that he happens to know
there's a Gowner dinner at a restaurant in Park Row
tonight.

"We'll be waiting outside when they toddle out
in their gowns pissed as farts.
Sober 'em up like. We'll nip round to
old Turner's first."

Ned knows it's *possible* for this to be a triumph;
whilst also knowing it won't be. *This*
is what Ned sleeps through.

The plan had been to paint with water-based paint
on the racing-green bonnet of the beautiful car
something as unfriendly as: 'Big Nose';
or 'This car = shit'; or 'Gowner = wanker'.
& leave it at that.

Neil brings a can of red water-based paint & two brushes.
But Ewan brings a large can of red gloss paint
& a Stanley knife.

"Gonna slash the tyres?" Neil asks. "No need mate."

"Not that, no."

They open both cans & Neil asks Ewan why he's bothering.

"You'll see," he says.

"Neil goes for 'Big Nose', at least an approximation to it as it's so dark.
Ewan adds a 'd' to 'Nose' and a word that *The Evening Post* will report
as being 'coward'. That wasn't the c-beginning word at all.
That done, Ewan takes out a Stanley knife, slides a blade
from the handle, locks the button in place and
then slashes through the canvas top of the cockpit
to expose to the night sky the gorgeous leather seats,
the polished wood steering wheel, the mahogany knob of the
gear-stick, the silver speed-dial & all the inner perfection onto which
he pours two pints of red gloss paint, sickening Neil
as it would anybody. It sends Ewan into ecstasies.

Now Neil feels ashamed & doesn't speak to Ewan unless he's
forced to. But he's been forced to cross a bridge into
a darker zone where shame is hard to locate among
the fatal 'in for a penny … ' thoughts. It's a harder form of
himself that waits across the road now from *Thatchers' Restaurant*
in Park Row clutching his mantis, as Ewan clutches his.

The focus now shifts to a different pair of friends, who both
live in Hotwells & will be staggering home together over
Cabot Hill past Cabot Tower at the end of the Gowner dinner.
They will have almost nothing to do with
the routine restaurant demolishing
as they are not keen on this, nor on Turner either —
who they see as dull & wet.
They are, though, lovers of their old school, of drinking,
a spot of light food-throwing, & shouted banter. They're not
the egregious thugs I've painted the Gowners as being.
Jacob was captain of rugby with all this entails —
bluff & tough, phlegmatic & laughter-loving. He's protective
of his friend — who's none of these things. Piers is delicate —
in short. Piers is just about the only one there tonight
who was a Scholarship boy. His parents are not well off;
he paid no fees because his 11+ results were so stellar.
Currently, he is in this final year at Oxford, expected to gain
a first in Greats. Just home for the weekend.

"Let's go for these two," says Ewan.

They're not the first out but they look like the easiest meat
so far.

Neil & Ewan trail them by a few yards as they cross
Park Street and walk up to Cabot Hill, fingers crossed
they'll take the short route across the park.
They do.

"We must go at the same time," whispers Neil.
But when Ewan sees Neil spray petrol on the hem
of Piers' gown then set a flame to it, he freezes,
lost in the conflagration. Jacob
doesn't seem to take it in, so drunk he is. He thinks
his friend has stepped on an ember & these two
guys have run up to help.

Neil presses the foam button & nothing happens,
presses & presses, throws the mantis away in fury,
shouts to the other two:

"Don't just stand there! Help me get his gown off."

Jacob obeys in a dream; but Ewan does not.
He still has his mantis
& his quarry: Jacob, who's doing all he can to help Neil.
He points the mantis at the hem of Jacob from behind,
but when he presses for petrol & flame nothing happens;
only the foam knob does its business as well as a
proper fire extinguisher.
Jacob is now black before & white behind.

"Aim it at this one you idiot," screams Neil,
"I can SMELL his legs burning."
Ewan continues as if the foam itself will be fatal to Jacob (it's the
successful functioning he seems to revel in).
At this point the true situation resolves to sense
in Jacob's rucked-up mind. In a second he turns and fells
Ewan with a blow in the face delivered with all his strength.
Milliseconds later he's back helping Neil.
But the combination of too-late-applied foam
& clothes ripping fails to prevent the terrible burning
Piers suffers.

A fine evening's work, then,
under the pristine snake-belts of the two Perry Comos:
a magnificent car pointlessly ruined in a diorama of how
stupidity & viciousness can intersect.

Second, a gentle young man with brilliant academic promise
is suffering from many third — & some fourth-degree burns.
His trauma will linger long after the burns are grafted over
& healed. His life is on hold, his parents & friends distraught.

Third, a younger man has had his nose destroyed &
suffered significant insult to the orbito-frontal
region of his brain. But Ewan will have the fame he craves:
as a substantial footnote to Phineas Gage's
more florid injury to that region. His mother will march up
to Latimer threatening to sue him for this 'neglect', but finds
solace in her son's medical distinction.
Neurologists look for the usual decrements
Ewan's moral sense & inhibitory control; but find little
evidence of actual *change*.

* * *

Always, Ned beats Lester Latimer at chess
when they have a lunchtime game, explaining after
where his boss went wrong; but today
he loses, lost in thought: no word from the lads
about last night. Then Lester says
as he winds up, flushed with success:

"These tree-lads from Mullens, weren't they mates of yours?"

The story comes out (yes, nabbed red-handed
for the paint-job too). Ewan's mum had phoned
Latimer first thing: shrill about his 'responsibilities here',
his being 'in local parentus', his 'allowing this to happen'.

Ned's first thought: they'll trace the mantises
back to me. But no, Neil told the police: "Oh, a pal
of mine brought these back from a holiday in Tangier.
They uses 'em for … Animal Husbandry over there see."

His second to twelfth thoughts are all about what his dad
will say & do.
If his dad phoned that day, maybe after reading *The Evening Post*
in Portishead, the game would be up.
In fact, Ed did try to phone but could not get through

as the line's dead now, thanks to the handiwork of Turner's
handy thugs, as said before. So why
did Turner trouble himself over such a
piddling act of spite?

Turner doesn't care much about the car, having
no feeling for machined beauty. He wanted
a Lotus & that's what he may well have now.
He doesn't give a damn about Piers, because, to him,
he is or was a peasant no less than the Ernies —
though his fulsome quote about him in *The*
Evening Post is this:
'Piers Bains was an exemplary Gowner, brave,
but sensitive, playful, yet fiercely intelligent.
We all loved him in our own particular ways'.

What's more, all this has been wonderful for
the Gowner public image. Never before have folks
felt anything like sympathy for a Gowner, & certainly
never for Martyn Turner. He can now imagine
continentally-dressed youths being spat at in the street
(they never were).

But the denominator of these three is his bubbling cauldron
of blind fury that 'This Kind of Thing Should Ever Happen
At All'. It happened at all
because of the Hales & they must be punished sorely.
How to punish them, he ponders?
How to tear right in half
this duo? Simple.
You work on Ned 'who's clearly as thick as a brick'.
You work on him by offering simultaneously
come-hither warmth (even a job offer?),
plus some explicit bombast of threat. He knows

he's actor enough to manage the former; but when
he aims for the latter he sounds more peevish

than lethal. His brother-in-law Nick Remplan
can fill that bill.
He'll coach him in the role.
It's hardly needed as he already spews out chest-beating
bullshit clichés about outsiders (not Bristolian
upper-middle class) at the drop of a hat. He'd love to be
a Gowner, this Merrywood Grammar boy.

But what a Godsend it is to Turner that Ed's stuck
in Portishead. The cut cable can isolate Ned further.
That's why …

Tea-time the next day & Ned is trying to accompany
a defeatist ballad sung by Edmund Hockeridge as he
prepares his beans on toast when there is a knock
on the maisonette door.
Remplan has forced an indigestive smile
& Turner is working up to a full Uriah Heap.
It has to be said that Turner's aims
are vague & emotion driven.
Good-cop/bad-cop might work when the aim is simply
confession, but there's no clear end-state here. He's clear
he wants to make Ned squirm & that he'll enjoy this a lot,
& perhaps he'll squirm away from his dad or away more
generally … so no not very clear at all.

TURNER: Oh, hello there Edwin. Can I call you Ned?
I do hope I'm not disturbing you. This is
my esteemed brother-in-law, Nick Remplan.

REMPLAN: Pleased to meet you.

NED: —

TURNER: Sorry but I really should have telephoned
first, but the line seems to be out of order.

NED: Yeah, what happened was —

TURNER: We called round for a number of reasons
& one was to say how sorry we are about
your friend. I have to admit to being a Gowner,
for my sins, but even as a Gowner I cannot defend
the rash action of Jacob Griffin. Thoroughly uncalled for.
He's a hothead. Can we come in?

[They enter.]

NED: Like a mug of orange squash? It's good
with hot water & a bit of sugar.

TURNER: That's so kind of you, but we
had some refreshments earlier.

REMPLAN: I could fancy a beer. D'you have any?

NED: Sorry, no.

REMPLAN: Don't suppose you can afford it on what
they pay you. Beans on toast for tea, eh? 'There's
posh' as the Welsh say.

TURNER: We had to take a taxi up here Ned, as my
car is suffering from ... er ... redness.

REMPLAN: It's ruined, mucked up, buggered up good
& proper.
*[As he speaks he tours the living room picking up
objects then putting them down contemptuously]*
The good news is, though, I can just imagine
the state of that Ewan McKann: strawberry jam
poured over a smashed dolly's face. Serves him right,
I say. He's vermin — & his mate. Why do you associate
with vermin, Mister Hale, Eh?

TURNER: I say, steady on Nick.

NED: I didn't know they'd do that to the car —

REMPLAN: So, you knew they'd do *something* then.
Do the police know about this?
God, what a tiny TV. You'd need a microscope
to watch Fabian on that.

NED: I don't like Fabian. Quite like Frankie Avalon though.

REMPLAN: I meant Fabian of Scotland Yard.
Christ!
Some mothers do have 'em.

TURNER: But 'I am not my brother's keeper'
as they say. These lads were hotheads Ned.
So, we have that in common: suffering by
our association with hotheads.
Can't be held responsible can we?
But I say, I was wondering where you dad is.
Or to put it another way
When—did—you—last—see—your—father?

REMPLAN: [*loud soto voce*] He won't get the reference Mart.
Not over-indulged with grey matter I'd say.

NED: He's in Portishead. His friend's motorbike
broke down so he's stuck there for a bit.

TURNER: Which spurs the questions: why is he there
& why consorting with motorbike types.

REMPLAN: Yes, one's who can't even be bothered to
maintain their bloody bikes properly.
Teds I expect.

TURNER: It's OK Ned. I was only joking
about the bike, as I'm sure Nick was too.

NED: Fair enough, would you like to sit down?

TURNER: Thanks mate. Oh, & isn't old Latimer
a bit concerned about your dad's absence?

REMPLAN: The old fart's past caring. Away
with the proverbials half the bloody time.

NED: I don't think that's very nice, Mr Remplan.
I think Lester's a really decent old chap.
Very good to me & dad. Not a bad
chess player too, though he's got a lot to learn
about putting an attack together.

REMPLAN: *[with genuine not manufactured passion this time; & still touring the flat picking up objects, never makes eye-contact with Ned]*
Oh, I say! Pardon me for breathing, I'm sure.
Didn't realise what a daycint owld chayp this
lovely gent was.
Aye shudah knowed what a daysint old stick he was.
Couldah knocked me dahn wiv a fevah.
Sorry Bambi, but who the hell
do you think you are to: A. take me to task about anything;
& B. have any bloody view at all on this *Bristolian* man.
Point is: what are you doing here at all,
the pair of you?
There's your dad who looks like a Maltese ponce
on the door of a strip club & you, a lumbering dogsbody.
Why did you ever leave London?
Your dear pappy was overheard saying he wanted
to put down roots in the West Country.
Don't you UNDERSTAND?
Roots aren't something you carry around in the hope
of planting them somewhere, like pitching a bloody tent.
Roots are something you either have or you don't,
like *character*.
Take your roots home — if you have one.

TURNER: It's OK Nick —

REMPLAN: I wish it was bloody OK.
London's just a dumping ground with shallow earth.
Fields of concrete. Can't put roots down there chum.
[He stalls, temporarily at a loss then …]
Take the darkies.
In Bristol, the darkies have their own … section.
St Pauls, that's where they live, apart from a few strays.
In St Pauls they can parade around in their baby-blue
suits & luminous ties then go home to their teas
of Kit-E-Kat & rice, so we all know where we are.
They can be bus conductors if they like & it's all
very fine — 'Here's your change boss, sorry about the farthings'.
But you go up to London & they're rub-a-dub, cheek-
by-jowl breathing you down all over the shop.
Darkies in business suits. Darkies & chinks getting
together in pubs that aren't *designed* for them,
with dominos & pickled eggs. There they are

sitting up like members.
They can be cheeky too, back-chat like one of us
& all in cockney; none of the Jamaican patter
you get down here.
You're just a white version of them.
Cuttings in the wrong pot. Cuckoos. Clothes & bikes
from 'the continong' … thinking you're chic
compared to us … *[stalls again]*
Lorraine. Lolly. What made your dad ever think
he could walk off with her? He's like one of those darkies
in the Deep South that seduces the wife of the plantation owner
in the mansion on the hill …

TURNER: You may be confusing the issue a bit here Nick.
Anyway, Ned —

REMPLAN: All I'm saying here is:
you're not suited. You don't fit.
You're a bad fit & you should
fuck off.
[He is covered in confusion, but continues to examine objects.
Meanwhile Ned looks more amused than anything else,
satisfied with Remplan's auto-humiliation]

TURNER: Sorry Ned. Nick does like to speak his mind
doesn't he?
But can I pick up on just one nail or pin or tack with
which Nick's hammer did make good contact?
The word 'dogsbody'.
It's a brutal word, but it carries the ring of truth.

NED: I like it here. Suits me.
I like this work.

TURNER: I'm glad you do, but … well … but the fact is
you're not only doing menial jobs around here,
but you're living in the shadow of your father.
He's an upstanding guy alright — & all's fair
in love & war & the rest — but don't you ever feel
you're being smothered, being kept as a kind of
satellite to him?

NED: No, I don't. Fact is —

TURNER: I mean, you obviously have great potential.
Why not think of striking out alone? I mean
do you *like* being out in all weathers,
getting soaked, sunburn, earth under your nails?

NED: Yes. It's healthy for one thing.

TURNER: But what about an executive job indoors,
taking decisions, phoning folks up, staff canteen,
dressing up to go to work,
pretty typists & more money?
As you may know, my father owns Brendon Laboratories:
the photographic processing outfit.
They have a big office up in Gloucester.
Dad says they could use a bright young blade like you.

NED: Fancy a game of darts?

TURNER: … I'd love a game Ned.

NED: Here you are then.

TURNER: What a lovely set of arrows.
These are arrows fit for a king.

*[Ned closes the sitting room door to reveal
a dart-board on the other side. All the time
Remplan is still touring the flat, picking things up]*

NED: Nearest the bull to start.

***[Remplan picks up a photograph of a girl
in ATS uniform]***

REMPLAN: Tell you what Mart … Here's one for you.
[*holding up the photo*] … What order did the Sergeant Major
never give when the ATS went on parade? ....
I'll tell you. 'Close up! Close up!' Door-ever-open girls
they were. Right bunch of scrubbers.

[This is a photo of Ned's mother during the war.]

"This one's passable though.
I'd shag it.
Not much for sale in the titty shop though —

For good reason did Remplan stop there.
At first, Turner thought that Ned had swiftly swatted
away a fly near Remplan's head.
In fact, he's thrown his dart into Remplan's face
with a severity that was sickening but balletic.
The point lodges in the middle of his forehead,
quivering there.   He is now stock-still
& white, a marble statue with staring eyes.
There's not much blood — a little.
Turner, too, is in shock — frozen for the moment.

"Off you pop, Turner," says Ned. "Get him out of here."

Ned, cold & martial, leaves first, going down into
the little back garden to fetch the hose.
This he aims at them as they stagger away, turning on the tap
full & squeezing the mouth of the pipe to
intensify the jet.

Soaked they move away slowly.

"This should wash the blood away," shouts Ned.
"Now you can get back to your friends all refreshed."

'This is what it feels like to be an animal',
is what Ned might have said — not the killer violence,
oh no: the perceiving-&-acting
without reflection.   Without daring a thought
he finishes
his cold beans-on-toast, drinks a pint of milk,
turns on the radio & mechanically tunes to
The Third Programme which is relaying
a concert by a string quartet. He endures
the 'scraping' & sits & sits & sits.
When he eventually goes to bed
he falls asleep at once.

In the dream that finally wakes him up he's watching
Neil & Ewan doing the split star jump in a shop window
until it's his turn.   He divides his nose
in the window corner till suddenly he can see himself.
What he sees
                    is his body being split in half
by a giant sword
from crown to crotch
over & over again.
He knows in dream-knowing that he is being
punished for allowing Turner & his allies
into their home, punished too for the blackness
of the dart intention, for letting that in him surface.

On waking, he allows in the facts of his
grotesquely naïve hospitality blunder
& the fact of his killing desires & vows
to shun all violence henceforward.
All his potential future violence was
compressed into that single act;
& he's finished with it now.

The breakfast of *Frosties* gives him a sugar rush.
He's free today. It's Saturday. Free too of his dad to
play whatever record he likes as *loudly* as he likes.
He slides from its sleeve his latest purchase, realised
just a few weeks ago & already his favourite, relegating Adam Faith.
He slides it out with care like an unexploded bomb:
Please Don't Touch, by Johnny Kidd & The Pirates.

He joins in the refrain at his fullest volume:

Please don't touch
I shake so much
Please don't touch
I SHAKE so much.

He dances too, threatening crockery.
The loud knocking at the door of the maisonette
he can just hear above the racket.

The man is smartly dressed, fresh faced,
with long fair hair curling over his ears.

"Detective Inspector John Archer [shows his ID]
Can I come in Mr Hale?"

Ned reverts to the 'animal' frame of mind from last night.

"I've just popped round to convey thanks
from the lads & lassies of the Neurology Department
of the BRI: thanks for all the 'frontal' lesions
you've had a hand in delivering to them recently.
They should get a good few research reports
out of them."

He's not like a policeman. More like
the brightest boy in the class who is also
the most turbulent. Yet he's benign, somehow.

"Seriously though, we have more than suspicions
here. Turner can't admit that his people have become
the victims of successful violence from you lot.
He *says* that Remplan just happened to walk in front
of your dart. Sure, if you'd been aiming at a board
50 yards away. Then there's the terrible twosome
& their dangerous toys. Your dad's got clever contacts &
you were their mate … & we have our theories here.
But look, we don't like the sodding Gowners any more
than you do & we don't like the idea of, lets call it,
tribal ructions in our city.

So, a word to the wise Mr Hale.
Stay away from violence.
Knock it on the head.
Keep calm.
No more fire & sharp points from you."

For reasons beyond him Ned now mimics an expression
he's heard from his co-workers in response to
the quoting of some
too-well-known fact; & he does it in convincing
Bristolian:

"OK skip. But tell us news, not history."

Ten: Nastiness Rising & Patsy Down

You're in a forest clearing sitting on a log,
not a pure clearing as the light is dappled,
more like a vertical tunnel tightly rounded
by thickly wooded trees, in late spring.

You are the calm recipient of private opinions
expressed in the mouths of trees,
whose voice is the wind.

It confuses you.

There is not one wind but three, each
from a slightly different direction:
as winds can be in a time-out dream.

The wind from the left
is constantly confidently insisting & while
you are far from the treetops it feels caressing.
You could also call it protective or maternal:
the voice of a dutiful mother pushing the trees
unwillingly to school firmly, gently.

It blows the case for the Edwins Hale:

"You call them interlopers, with alien values & tastes
when they are working men only, struggling
along a hard road …
Ed is upstanding, principled, a good father
(OK, indifferent husband, so not quite the 'pious family man'),
strong when he needs to be, intelligent too —
a leader & a doer above all.

Must those who make their way within the shuffling
columns & hand-to-mouth of lower London be destined
to do so forever?
Do the soft contours of the West *belong* to those who happen
to live there now (& don't many of those
despise Western ways?)
It's clear
his work is unfinished.
The work of him & Lolly is unfinished & potential.
He did not 'steal' her from Martyn Turner.
I don't even *need* to make the case for that.
Ed is the *recipient* of violent opposition.

He has a style, a self-chosen one
that happens, by God-given chance,
to line up with that of a cohort
variously called continentals, or modernists
by the Gowners modricks.
He does not seek them as allies.
Social & aesthetic forces meld them.
So much is out of his hands.
I admit he took steps
to ally himself with the Teddy Boy faction;
but what choice does he have?
Must he roll over & be kicked to pieces
by posh delinquents?
I admit, too, he is superstitious with a weakness
for the lurid fancy that destroys confident drift;
but this has diminished. When do we hear
of Ioanna now?
The *I Ching*? It's only the religion of the gambling mentality;
& it only 'tells' him what he already knows.
His leaning on his mother?
Part & parcel of his familial piety, I would say.
But *what* can I say
to defend his son?
Grandmotherly feelings are not those

of a diluted mother.
I see him as others do — a Woolworths
pick-&-mix counter of threads of some man's character.
Oh, who would match the child-like dolt with
the Incredible Computing Prodigy, or with
the Avenging Angel Lethal with Sharp Points?
I just know that now I love him, where
I used to try to forget who he was … "

At this the wind dies down.

From the right comes another feminine breath,
not in the slightest bit maternal, with something
of the headmistress regretting (really not at all)
that it's her stern duty to deliver an upshot
in hard sudden gusts.
There is a lull.
The shadowed leaves on the ground
are as still as the pattern of a rood screen.
Then, as if the trees are being punished, slapped down,
or as if they know
this wind is the harbinger of something worse
& they're running to escape, the hard wind comes.
It comes with a high buzz-saw of complaint.
Oh, this is a friend of the family alright:
a friend of a different family — the Turner family,
a stiffener of all the strings
that bind the moneyed layer to the Gowners,
marbled & buttressed with Clifton stone:

"Edwin Hale is a stone thrown into a pool.
Its surface, once glassy black, now throbs & bucks.
The centre is pure turbulence with reeds & small creatures
being slapped again & again against a depressed bank.
Where there was a delicate ecology
of competing but complementary interests
there is chaos & destruction, all thanks to this 'upstanding' man.

'Stone' I say …
He's about as much of an agent as that:
not strong but resilient & hard & mentally dull.
How can you be strong when you are stone-inert?
He's only an agent of his borrowed imaginings
while agents in reality act on him & he is
their stone-agent.

He let Dana fall in love with him,
let himself be swilled away by his fancies, fuelled
by something that's no more than petal-plucking & coin tossing.
As for Martyn & Lorraine, who is he
to turn his stony gaze
towards his importunate speech or her reluctance?
It's their coupledom & their business!
He's just the stone that poor Lester Latimer
plucked from a beach in his limp way.
He saw the slightly rough but smooth no-nonsense surface
veined with what he thought he needed
& put him to work & then himself to bed.
& while he lies in bed Ed places his great feet
under their table
in the role of a roughly-competent diamond
scratching outlines of Lambrettas
on their suburban glass.

Everything was glassy clear before he made it
a clear distortion. Yes, there is an arrogance
in Martyn; he makes the most of his privilege
& he can be off-kilter in his speech in this way & that.
But he can be looked up to.
He is, after all, the President of the Gowner Dining Club.
& Gowners, though they have their own roughness,
are *intelligent & educated*. They chose him.
Being a leader suits him; he's been brought up to it.
Hale is a leader through craft & ingratiation.

Listen! Do you want a levelled-down world?
A world in which hard-nut dandies who carry
bicycle chains & razors, & lower-order style-hounds
who mimic the epiphenomena of whatever
they think they ought to like call the shots?
Do you want a world where robbery is legal?
Where people who merely want to keep
what's theirs must join
the back of every queue?
A world where upper-class thuggish-ness is thought evil,
but the lower-class version is held up as evidence of
a rich sub-culture?
Do you think,
do you really think
that those in the upper tier will say 'help yourself'
when yahoos try to take what's theirs?
They'll fight back with a vengeance so fierce
this will never be tried again
in any other corner.
& who, by the way,
would they fight against?
A man who is nothing in himself,
whose only skill is pointing out steadily & dully,
like the stone statue he is,
how unfair it is that the rich exist at all
to those who dress up & cavort
in the pockets & broad domains of wealth created
by bold men who live by risk!"

This wind ends deceptively, stopping
suddenly, pausing long, & then giving
a final mad blast, then nothing for five minutes
after which …
a middle-wind starts up — masculine;
this time old, rightly assuming that
the left & the right women are competing for his ear.
He's telling them what he's 'minded' to do.

He is minded to do nothing much, to let
the forces — such as they are —
fail to cohere & play themselves out.
You could say his heart is with the maternal left,
but his astute old intellect fears what the right-woman
says is already taking place —
a conflict of upper & lower classes.

Imagine a city riven with such a division!
he tells us. Not quite saying (he's an aristocrat himself)
"You can't just mow them down or cut them down these days
& they have the numbers.
It would be Goodbye Bristol as we know it."
You may appreciate that
the only thing impeding this now
is (what I call) Ernies' dislike of Ed.
But if they turned this against Turner
we'd have something easy to imagine
that once seemed as impossible as two symmetrically
opposing winds: class war!

How can this mild middle man engineer it away?
By letting the muddle muddy itself with contingency
& the actors' various incompetencies.
As the right wind says: Ed does not
really know what he's doing beyond
some misty dream of 'finding a home'.

But right now Ed knows exactly what he's up to
as he parks the scooter outside the maisonette
& helps down Patsy from the pinion.
He's on his way to giving Ned a piece of his mind.

        This is a new Ed,
        or maybe a regurgitated older one.
It's more than anger. It's more
as if he's suddenly been faced with a reality

he must deal with: the extreme sour
seriousness this gives rise to.
Of course,
he lectures Ned on his stupidity in befriending
'those nasty little twerps'
& allowing Turner into their home.
"What where you thinking?"
when he aimed that dart at Remplan's face.

Well, if he wasn't thinking then,
he is certainly not thinking now
of a word his dad is saying.
He's immune from any other force
having met the force of Patsy.

There she is, smiling in her pink jeans,
blowing a bubble, filing her nails.
He knew she was coming & had imagined
a mannish lump with a hula hoop.
But this!
It's all he can do to turn his mind from the crackling
electricity between his father & her.
But nothing is relevant to his complete surrender
to her.

"Very pleased to meet you. Fancy a game of pontoon?"

"Maybe later," as Patsy looks through his record collection
& admires his Dansette. "Hey, I see you've got the new
Johnny Kidd."

"I'll put it on."

"Oh no you won't," says his dad who proceeds
with self-conscious manliness to explain
'the rules of the house' (mostly about use
of the bathroom).

Patsy, herself, seems very focussed on
what she should buy & cook for their meals
& puts on her serious face for this.
It's only a face: she is never fully serious,
levity always round the corner.

Oh, she both delights & disturbs them.
She is a good cook & energetic cleaner.
One day she spends all afternoon making
a beautiful dessert with strawberries, apricots,
whipped cream, drizzled chocolate, marzipan,
dense moist cake, the lot.
"Wonderful but why?" they say.
"Because it's my birthday."
"But we haven't bought you a present!"
"You paid for the ingredients gentlemen."
The next day Ed makes for a jeweller's in the High Street
& buys an eccentrically pretty necklace —
thin brushed steel with a string of glass beads
like electric wine gums.
She wears it all the time, always.
She is happy & makes them happy despite
both men being in love with her
in their different (not *completely* different)
ways … leading to one face of the 'disturbing'.

When things settle down a bit Ed lets Ned play
Please Don't Touch, at which with less than a second's pause
Patsy jumps up to dance: a shaking free-form dance,
more African than not.   Both men
shake innerly.
On her second day there, a Sunday morning,
she asked if she can have a bath. Of course!
Both men sitting throughout this, Ed pretending
to listen to *The Archers*, Ned pretending to read
The Sunday Express:
both men thinking-imagining the same thing

& each knowing this of the other.
Then … how can you fail to recognise someone
you are in love with?
But they do.
Back from the bath, no make-up for the first time,
hair falling in dark wet curtains, wearing a big sloppy-Joe
pullover; such purity, innocence, such disturbing joy.

The next area of disturbance is more to our point.
As her father George promised, Patsy has
many contacts among the Teds in this North-end of the city
& they are a lary lot, even for Teds.
"No," she tells them, "no slashers & chains;
it's not that kind of thing. Embarrass Gowners in the street,
make life difficult for them, show them up."

Their way of doing so involves shouting & tripping up.
Or things like this:
confusing actual Gowners with boys in the QEH
6th form who are often seen drifting down Park Street.
They like to walk one each side of a lad, lift him up
by the arm-pits & bellow in his ear:
'PRICK, THE BANDIT!'
The Teds enjoy this a lot.

Now, for the deepest disturbance of all.
Patsy has an idea.
She's heard that a big Gowner dinner —
a centenary of some kind — is to be held
at the *Mauritania* restaurant between the bottom
of Park Street hill & College Green.
She's also heard that some new offensive
is being planned — against the Hales & against
both Teds & 'modricks' more generally.
Already there have been fresh assaults, via
the usual handy thugs, on their home (the external
stop-cock turned off early morning & tea-time frequently,

three times cod loins writhing with maggots have been pushed
though an under-floor air-brick to stink the place out).

Patsy sees her mission as finding out
what is being planned. They will surely discuss
(i.e., scream across tables) this at the dinner.
So … she intends to get a job waitressing at the dinner
(again, her contacts help) …
"But they'll recognise you!" (Ed, desperate)
"Wait, I just do this." She fetches a blonde-bob wig
puts it on her head & says:
"Zay will neverrr recognise-a me. My name ees Claudia."

Two kinds of disturbance here for the price of one.

The day arrives & Ed tells Patsy
to telephone from the *Mauretania* at 10.00 pm
to tell him how things are going.
"OK, if I can."
"Do it!" Desperate Ed again. The new Ed.

The *Mauretania* is not like the usual Gowner venue —
large, late-Victorian, functional, more like a pub
& patronised often by the working classes who've saved up
for a special occasion. You might see
two office boys in their best suits
having *Wills Whiff* cigars with their after-dinner port,
feeling superior together, for once.
Are the Gowners out in force for some reason?
Is it the closeness to the Centre & gathered 'Modricks'?
Who knows & who cares when the clock shows
10.15 & no word yet … at last.

"Ed?"

"What's up? Are you OK?" Ed does not give a damn
about the Gowners' plans.

" … Yes, but it's getting a bit lively here."
A gruff male voice: "Get off that bloody phone &
look lively … [inaudible]"

"As I said, all a bit *lively*." Sound of breaking glass.
"Look, my boss says if I don't get on with it he'll
send me home & I haven't found out … Whoops … bye."

Ned is awake & wants to go with his dad
when Ed sets off at midnight.

12.25: The place is in semi-darkness because
of smashed light-bulbs. But there is an air
of positive buoyant industry as they clear up.
No sign of Patsy.
& none of the waiting staff seems to have heard of her.

Eventually, he finds the manager —
a smiling satisfied man, whom Ed detests immediately.

"Your place is wrecked."

"Oh yeah, but they left a cheque for £1000 to cover damages
& the insurance will take care of it on top of that,
plus loss of business for a couple of days,
so a pretty good night all round."

"I'm looking for a waitress called Patsy."

"No one by that name mate."

[The penny drops …] "She may call herself Claudia."

"Oh, her. They liked her — in their way [snigger].
She must have popped off early — sort of vanished
about eleven-ish."

Ed runs off asking staff about Claudia,
randomly opening doors, cupboards, looking
behind the bar, with blood in his eye …

"Clowdial? Oh, she … well you know …
was a bit lively. Yer mind?"

It's a kind of pantry where they keep tablecloths,
candlesticks, cutlery, a few cheese wheels.
In the corner on the floor
a small disarrangement of body
with a blonde wig half-covering a face
& a pair of white knickers half-covering
a twisted foot in a black court shoe.
"NO," she screams as Ed leans over her in tears
"NO!"
Her face is white & after that she is mute
shaking & staring — mute.

Ed phones 999 for ambulance & police.
Finds the manager & punches him in the belly
with every ounce of his force.
Does the same to all men in authority who *seem*
to be withholding something about "Claudia" —
she whom they "liked, in their way."
When the police arrive they find a number of men
doubled up on the floor clutching their stomachs:
some vomiting, all moaning.

"Come down with a bit of food poisoning then
did they?" jokes Sergeant Ham.
They don't care about the men.
They do care about the assaulted girl —
rape? attempted rape at least.

Sergeant Ham has just missed Ed's spree of violence —
better 'spasm', or 'explosion' —

from which women were not exempt …
Just a snigger at the name Claudia & they'd be thrown to the floor.
Few men were safe: the head chef made a joke
& said "problay she flirted with 'em."
It was enough for Ed to garnish the belly punch like this:
stomps with his boot-heels on the fingers of both
his hands — such a satisfying crunch.
"Happy cooking fatso," was his farewell.

This new kind of Ed did not subside.

He hears the verdict is 'attempted rape' &
cannot bear to think what 'attempt' means.
Thinks only on the violence that's owing.
Culprit or culprits?

'Elective mutism' is the diagnosis — a feature of her 'shell-shock' …
She spends her days now in Barrow Gurney mental hospital
in the rural outskirts of South Bristol.
Ed, Ned & her father are the only men she will allow into
her room; when alone she shrinks into the wall.
Usually curled like a shellfish into herself,
screened with drugs, silent, & less than a quarter of herself.

Ed visits her only with Lolly (two men is one too many).
His violence project will not allow him to love
the Somerset beauty of the Barrow Gurney village
or the perfection of the tiny old pub
called *The Ich Dien* (or *Prince's Motto*).
They sit outside with their drinks before a gentle hill
& a small-holding with chickens.
The sweet & ancient landlady, Mrs Patch, politely asks
Ed if he will move his scooter a little to one side
to make room for a fourth car in the car park …
He snaps & bristles with rubbish about 'my custom' …
'can't see any cars on the horizon' … 'all in good time
missus.'   Lolly cannot stand it &

crosses the road to look at the chickens
leaving Ed to spit beer through his teeth
at the fender of an Austin A30,
like a minor Ted.

You could say violence is channelled under all his activity;
but that's not quite right.
There is an urge to destroy in his deep,
which curdles as it funnels up
to something like the sour pomposity
of an English tourist abroad with a jippy tummy.
          He's noted on his last visit to Patsy
          that she's not wearing her birthday necklace &,
          all his intelligent reflection gone, his first thought
          is that somebody in the hospital has stolen it.
Ned is near to tears when he hears
his father on the phone to the hospital:
polite at first, then: "So, I am forced to conclude
that you have LIGHT-FINGERED EMPLOYEES.
The constabulary will show an interest, no doubt.
Heads will roll, I can assure you of that."
          Ned watches
as his father replaces the receiver,
almost with satisfaction.

He is a warrior who needs to rage around
with a slashing sword; while the modern world
reduces him to this?   Well …
that's the generous reading.

There is nothing and something of the warrior
in how he deals with old Frank Menzies,
a worker of failing knees & bull neck.
Frank has worked on the estate nearly all of his adult life,
essentially a stone mason who now turns his hand
to any hard surface, a widower who lives
in a bespoke cottage on the estate
with his son Laurie. Laurie is lively, though a shade simple.

It's now getting close to the Goram Fair
& Ed wants father & son to carry stones
from a defunct rockery in the garden
to build a grotto near the Goram giant where folks
can keep an eye on their kids clambering over
its legs & enjoy a cuppa and a cake from the nearby stall.
He wants it built to his own design.
Their progress is slow & Ed complains
in his newly hateful manner.

One day Frank catches up with Ed
(difficult in his new feverish state) & tells him straight
that his design is not only 'a bit daft' but 'dangerous
especially if there's kiddies around'.
"Fact is boss, you don't understand.
You can't just put stones on top of one another.
You need proper plans & a support structure;
& the cementing will look ugly done your way.
& it's — sorry — a blinking waste of our time
to cart them stones half way across the estate.
The old rockery looked dandy how it was,
past its best, of course, but people like it well enough.
A fox lives there, doing no harm."

"Foxes spread rabies, you old fool."

"No they don't."

"Silent! If I wanted your aesthetic & architectural judgements
I'd have damned well asked for them. Look,
I'm having the devil of a time booking the helter-skelter &
the shooting ranges & in you shuffle with this
cock & bull. Do what you're paid to do man.
If you're too old to do the carrying then you can watch
your genius of a son do it.
& as for the fox, shoot it! Poison it!
Get rid of it toot sweet."

Frank is literally cap-in-hand, the rim of his flat cap
circuiting through his stubby fingers.

"I made an objection to you & you've not even tried
to answer it. Can I speak about this to somebody
who's, like, in the know?"

"Get out!"

Frank walks, or seems to crawl, away;
not humiliated, but feeling he's entering
a new horrible domain that's nothing
to do with him & cannot touch him.
Back at their cottage Frank relays it all
to Laurie. The next morning Laurie is up
at first light to move all the stones back
to the rockery.
Now it's Ed's turn to do some catching up,
finding Laurie applying cement
to loose flints on the folly.

"Well?"

"I moved 'em back boss.
You should not of spoken to dad like that.
Just not; it's not fair. Everybody knows
he's right & you're wrong … Them stones
belong in the rockery. Sorry boss!"

"You're sacked. Call in to the office
& collect your cards before lunchtime.
You don't work here anymore Menzies."

This is less than a tragedy for Laurie Menzies
as it should be easy to find another job locally.
But it's a deep wound to his father.

But there is almost an air of relief
about Frank. He is distressed, but
somehow happy to be forced to accept
the reality of this rock bottom.

"I've come to hand in my notice Mr Hale."

"You what!"

"I don't want to work here anymore."

For once the new Ed falls away to reveal a vulnerable man —
visible in his eyes.

"You'll lose your home. You'll have nowhere to live.
You're cutting your own throat Frank."

"I don't care, tell you the truth. I'd rather for us
to be homeless for a bit than have to work for you.
My son's a good lad.
You're a father & you give him the sack
for sticking up for *his* father."

Ed sits down heavily in the nearest chair.

"I'm so sorry, Frank."

But the old man is too far away to hear him by now.

Back in the forest it's a windless night,
cold & dark & it's Ed himself,
not you
sitting on the damp log,
looking up to where he knows still trees are,
praying for the dawn to come
& wishing there were something
he could do to make it come sooner.

Here he is, the victim of turbulence:
inner & outer.
Nobody could be less like the 'stone'
he was accused of being.

Eleven: From 'Frances Drake' to 'A Dangerous Girl'

Dawn breaks to show the log occupied,
not by Ed, but by Lester Latimer — as if
he's been sent there by the headmaster to contemplate
all of his fallings short.   This time these are not
speaking winds: they're winds that evoke
two frames of mind in the sitter just as tunes
call out emotions.

One wind, a shade to the left, is gentle
& warm; the trees hardly stir but lean steadily forward
as if listening out for something.
It reminds Lester of his kindliness & strength,
of his bold imagination when he took to Ed & trusted him,
his generosity of spirit in building the confidence
of Ed's son over the chess board & his acuity
in seeing where the lad's talents really lie
(much more of this much later).

Above all, it evokes his boldness & paternal piety —
confronting the thunderous fury of his wife —
in allowing his daughter to follow her heart.
                    Earlier I called him a rock. I know I added
he was 'worn away' by events, but rock certainly.
It was wearing, yes, but he could withstand — & he knows
he can withstand — the waves of resentment crashing
against him from all sides. He could be worn, but never
washed away.

A visitor to his home might say he is under the thumb
of his wife. But what powerful man is not?
It's the little men who are domestic tyrants.
                    In this frame

he is clearly on Ed's side & has been seen to be
all along.
Something in Turner makes him shudder
while there is a comfortable rightness about Ed
& his world, well-earthed though nicely off-kilter.

But what are those steadily leaning trees listening for?
For the fierce truth-telling of the second wind,
clearly from the right —
hard & gusting, howling & cold.
Here it comes.

It's nonsense that Lester is really on the side of the Hales!
All he has done is to employ him, for his own convenience,
exercising his own political sense
in letting Lorraine have her head.
As this wind's right-direction colleague pointed out,
the dispute & all the mess of it now have the flavour
of class war.   All depends on that.
                             To Latimer, Ed is a
                             peasant,
a useful peasant who speaks their language
with useable peasant hardness. His daughter
is surely no peasant & she'll soon tire
of him when she sees the light …
The scenario is so, so familiar.
                      Pretty posh girl
falls bodily for a dangerous greaser
& two weeks later she's cringing as he drinks
her father's Margaux like it's beer ('noice
drop a woin this squire'); he oils the lawn black
with motor-bike innards, he's dull …

Latimer is, deep in his hidden mind,
on the side of Martin Turner by necessity & fate.
Yes, he's Oxbridge where Turner is commercial;
yes, Turner's manner grates on him a lot;

but he is in the broader sense family.
His wife's manner grates on him too; but he's on *her* side,
the family side. In short, he's married to the Turner side
& that's the fact to deal with.

What do you think Latimer does in his spare time?
Goes down the pub for a pork pie & a pint?
Does the washing up to the strains of Winifred Atwell's
rendition of *The Poor People of Paris* on the *Light Programme*?
He goes to dinner with people like Percy Turner,
Martyn's father.   He and Anita dress up,
take a taxi; they sit in the garden before dinner,
enjoying an aperitif, listening to faint zoo-sounds
(squawks, roars, the proto-language of primates,
maybe a trumpet or two) drifting across on the air.
                    Sometimes they will take Lorraine with them
&, indeed, Martyn may drift in for a glass before heading out.
Watch the two of them together.
Not a natural couple, no, but they swim
in the same waters of social form.
They can chat disinterestedly & lightly.
He can stimulate her social laugh.
It's clear he has a real wit, not only
the joshing cruel kind but a dry
deflating narrative that clears the air of pretension.
The two of them could become friends, maybe
even 'try again' when she sets this in her mind
against the embarrassing almost non-verbal
aw-shucks-mam of the hired cowpoke that
Ed really is.

Ed Hale is never fun; Martyn can be fun.
Latimer knows this & Latimer is on Martyn's side,
so this wind tells him.
Why else do you think he failed to endorse fully their marriage plans?
It's not that he's 'taken to his bed'.
He's a politician who knows where he naturally stands;

knows when to withdraw.   Latimer looks at Ed
& sees a profoundly un-intelligent man. Does this person
really believe that support for peasants can come
from anything other than *peasants*?

Some say that this is not really a brewing class war at all
& give the case of the Ed-hating Ernies; but Ernies
don't count
& never have or will.
Need it be added
that Latimer knows about the demeanour of the new
nastier Ed? He knows all about the Menzies affair,
which is no more than two peasants
fighting in a sack.
Of course, the bigger peasant bit off the other's head.
Well, fine: it's what peasants do in their gross, lumbering,
pissed-off way.

When the Goram fair is finished & he's supervised
the clearing up & paid all the bills it will be
goodbye Hales, sink back to your level,
the building-site beckons.

There is no third wind between, but
something from the earth.
He gazes down at the scrubby grass,
the leaf shadows, dandelions, daisies,
an earwig climbing a grass blade & feels
his God-like position. He feels the weakness
in wind one, feels strong, strong shame at wind two,
feels the potential in himself to act.
'For God's sake', the earth says, '*act*'!

Dawn arrives differently for Ed:
he's not pondering his divided self
but undergoing the fact of his recent awfulness
& longing to escape from under it.

He knows he is really a *gentle*-man & will strive
to manifest this again. But 'strive'?
How can he do this?
Take her father, Georgios Eviades, as a model.
Patsy is his daughter while she was his *housekeeper*
of two weeks acquaintance; & yet he has gone sour
with despair & George wears a simple, sad dignity.
What's more, he's never offered a word of blame
towards Ed, when obviously Ed should have made her
stay home that night (let's face it, he didn't want
to upset her); he'd learn their plans soon enough.
Quite: ENOUGH of this maundering in
reference-letter phrases over the obvious.

Ed has arranged a drink with George at a venue
of his own choosing. He chooses *The Hen & Chicken*
in Southville. Ed is a few minutes late;
no sign of George. Surely not!
That old fellow in the corner is *him*?
He's come straight from his job
as a removal man wearing an ancient grey suit
& collarless shirt. He could be
a butcher's assistant fallen on hard times.
The greatest absence is his hair-style no longer
exceeding its grasp: the Ted pompadour-scaffolding
has gone, replaced by an OK-I-give-up comb-over —
making, with his side-burns, a face wider
than it is high …

After Ed sits down George's first words are …

"It's all bollocks isn't it?"

It turns out he means (what could be called) the tribal violence
is bollocks: of the pointless, relentless plain-stupid variety.
He could have added that violence may be a hobby
for the upper classes, but it's a necessity of life

when you've got to fight to maintain yourself
at the lower level.
                    Ed, haltingly,
tries to heap blame on himself for letting Patsy
go to the *Mauretania,* but George says …

"There's no telling her Ed.
She's a stubborn little cow."

At the last phrase Ed sees a tear in his eye.

Two pints later they agree that the way to end
the 'bollocks' is for Ed & Turner to square off,
just the two of them, resolve the issue into
one final battle.
                    But 'battle' sounds absurd.
So far, 'battle', 'blood', 'fight' and so on
have been metaphors for summary nastiness —
often more symbolic than real. To have a *real* fight
would be like taking a joke in earnest.
Later, somewhat drunkenly, Ed suggests
having Ned bring the Dansette into the hospital
& playing *Please Don't Touch* in the hope it will
awaken her old self.

"Don't be a stupid tart Ed. That part of our Pats
is gone for good. May as well try to wake the dead.
It's in in the past mate."

After a long silence, George mutters something in Greek.
        They part
        on good terms,
planning their next drink in *The Ich Dien*.

So what of the 'action' that Lester has promised himself?
He hits upon a plan which,
like many of his plans, would involve talking things over

in his 'morning room or sun lounge.'
The basic idea is a good one:
have a figure of status along from the QEH
to politely, but firmly, undermine
the ethos & rationale of the Gowners Dining Club
to Martyn Turner.
He knows
that if their 'dinners' ceased, or were toned down
to sedate affairs, some essential poison would be drawn.

It's very unlikely he would have thought this
had not public opinion turned so sharply against the Gowners
post the Patsy attack. This opinion was fuelled by
The Evening Post.   A few words
about this local paper. It comes out every evening plus
the '*Pink 'Un*' on Saturday for the sport.
Its editorials are solidly anti-Gowner,
while its fashion editor is something of a modernist
himself: devoting whole pages to the button-down collar,
the long narrow shoe, the stacked heel & 'parallel' trousers.
But most important, each week they have an update on
Patsy with photographs. For example, they may show her stooped
in the Barrow Gurney gardens supported by two female
members of staff plus the caption 'Aftermath of
a jolly Gowners' dinner'.

The Gowners' guns must be spiked,
he tells himself privately in his firm voice.

Now Dr St John Drake does not look like
or sound like a spiker of guns. Indeed, he looks & sounds
like somebody who could not bear to go near such things.
He used to be the Head of English at QEH & is now
a 'Adjunct Lecturer' in English at the University.
More important, he is the Deputy Head of Governors
of the school. He's QEH through & through & so,
Lester thinks, he's somebody to whom Turner

would listen & defer.
He also knows that Drake is a sceptic about Turner,
having taught him. In fact, he has
no idea how deep Drake's hatred for Turner goes.

But his biggest mistake is thinking that Turner will
respect Drake. Nothing could be less true.
To Turner, Drake is a soft old-woman who couldn't
control his classes or hold their attention,
who backs down almost as a policy.

It has to be said that Drake is interesting.
What makes him is his extreme articulacy.
If you saw a transcript of his general conversation
you would think it had been professionally edited
for publication. He speaks in paragraphs & there is
a thread of subtle, though often mimetic, wit running through.
There is too the kind of calm that marries so well
with verbal style & pose.   But when
you listen to him, it's far less impressive.
His voice is weak, the gaze unsteady; there is
an unconfident tone.

Similarly, if you'd seen photographs of him along
with the transcripts you would be impressed.
He carries off
the two-tone shirt (frequently a magenta torso
& cream collar) well. His hair is pure white, brushed
subtly forward like a drift of snow. His profile is
aquiline, & as if carved & polished.

He is a Catholic convert whose literary scholarship
begins & ends with Catholic & High Church authors.
All else is dull to him.
He gives a special course at the University (sparsely attended)
on the poetry of John Henry Newman. Indeed,
if you wanted to fix an image of him
it would be Newman in his Cardinal years.

Drake & Turner make Lester nervous
for different reasons: Drake because
of his long silences, staring into the far distance (maybe
planning a trio of vocal paragraphs) & his general delicacy;
& Turner because of his sharp joshing tongue
& general ungovernability.

Predictably, Drake is here first, turning down the offer
of coffee & slightly requesting "Earl Grey or white tea
if you should have it." They discuss the glory
of the flowers in Lester's garden, the view, & the weather;
then Turner turns up.

TURNER: Morning gents. Both looking very well this morning,
I must say.

DRAKE: Thank you so much.

LESTER: So do you Martyn.

TURNER: No I don't. I look a mess. & I feel hot & bothered
& very keen to get this over & done with as quickly as possible.

LESTER: You two know each other of course.

TURNER: Of course … of *course [with a sharp glance at Drake].*

DRAKE: If I recall aright the last time
we set eyes on each other was —

TURNER: Oh, can't we just get ON with it.

LESTER: Indeed … The fact is Martyn, the argie-bargie
that started when Ed Hale arrived on the scene — let's
not get tangled up in the reasons for this shall we? —
has resulted in — how to put this? — a kind of
spasmodic not-quite conflagration in which
the Gowners are both targets of hatred from some quarters
& the perpetrators of some really quite bad behaviour.
We were all disgusted
by the attack on that unfortunate girl at your last

dinner Martyn & the fact is ... I mean to say
that fact is ... that many men of good will
feel that the Gowners' wings should be clipped.
Look, why can't you just
have dinners *[sniggers hopefully]*
'within the meaning of the act' —
a few drinks, a bit of the rough banter that we all enjoy,
some singing, rugby songs even, & then going home peacefully
to your beds in a sociable glow of wine, as it were.

TURNER: We could yes. So, what's your point exactly?

LESTER: The Gowners need to have their wings clipped
or else the whole city & much of the country will turn
against one of this city's finest schools, perhaps the finest.

TURNER: & Why should our wings be clipped? Why not
the 'wings' of razor gangs or the 'wings' of bum-boys
in bum-freezer jackets with little fringes of hair who park
their scooters on the pavement. We live in a free country Lester.
If some folks — some *peasants* say — in Bristol & elsewhere
wish to judge our school on the basis of what a bad apple
or two MAY have done then take pity on them.
It's a free country Lester.
[He drops his voice in a show of sadness]
It is really sad about that girl who disguised herself
as somebody called Claudia — Why do that by the way? —
But frankly who knows what actually happened;
she's not telling; and she seems *[heavy irony]* to have
lost her tongue.
By the way, is there any actual *evidence* that is was
one of our members?
I can recall a couple of randy-looking roughnecks serving us
... & some of these yobbos I saw in the kitchen!

DRAKE: If I may just interject at this point—

TURNER: Of course, you may Frances, don't be shy.

LESTER: Dr Drake's Christian name is St John Martyn,
as I thought you would know, not this 'Francis'.

DRAKE: It's alright Lester.

TURNER: Not Francis — Frances, with '... es.' I should pronounce it
Franceez.

LESTER: I still don't —

DRAKE: Really, it's alright Lester.

TURNER: When we were lively little hoodlums in his class
we used to have the nickname 'Frances Drake' for him,
like a wife for the famous mariner … It helped relieve
the tedium of the *Wreck of the Deutschland.*
Now what was it you were thinking of interjecting
St John?

DRAKE: *[brewing anger]* Just this & I'll say it with express
before adverting to the impertinence of your naming.
You use the phrase, vocally underlined,
'lost her tongue', use it with the clear implication
that she is withholding information rather than being
unable to give it, information about her attackers,
& this you imply, given your further views,
with the intent of directing blame onto your members
& away from one of her fellow workers.
But this young lady
is in extreme mental torment.
She is terrified. She has been
profoundly wounded in spirit, long term
or even permanently.
Meanwhile, you focus
on the precious freedoms owing to the members
of your seedy dining club. They are a disgrace
to the school, Turner. Already they drag it down —
not through the nether winds of public opinion,
but through the spiritual filth that is your element
You act as if you were the flower of an army fighting
for the values of our ancient school. I suppose
you believe that your manners are a harking back
to something as medieval as the school's origins —

TURNER: Of for God's sake, Frances. Why all this fannying
about? Where's your famous eloquence? None of this
makes any sense.

DRAKE: Will you kindly cease calling me Frances.
You aren't in school now.
No, in fact you are; as you are no more
than an overgrown schoolboy.
You love this absurd 'dining club' so much because it keeps you
at school.

You hide behind
it & protect its rotten elements because
they are like you: nasty, cruel, & bullying.

LESTER: Gentlemen, can we please lower the temperature
& keep to the subject at hand. This is not the way forward.
Martyn, do you not at least recognise that the dining club
is undergoing an ugly phase?
There has always been an element of thuggishness around
its edges, but look at what you're doing now:
playing down a clear case of rape.

TURNER: Clear? I wouldn't say so. Look at how much of
this is UNclear! Do we know anything of this girl's medical history?
Maybe she's one of these hysterical types. Maybe she's one of those —
what do you call them? — players-up, no, *role-players*.
What was she doing trying to pass herself off as a blonde
foreigner? I bet it's what hysterics do. Actually,
I wouldn't put it past her to have staged the whole thing.
No, better: she went into the cupboard with one
of the gypos who do the washing up & it got
out of hand.
Or ...
the whole thing was set up to harm the Gowners.
A conspiracy got up by those commies from *The Evening Post*.

DRAKE: I was going to say, Turner, that you have
a touch of evil in you. That's not so.
You are evil *at the core*.
I think I saw this early on, in fact.
I recall your scheming face in my class as you rocked
on your chair at the back, planning to inflict
pain of some kind on somebody, perhaps
on myself as one too defenceless & benign
for your tastes — or on one of your peers.
There are bad people, of course, but
they are not necessarily evil. Their bad-doing
may be caused by nothing more than
a fatal combination of the wrong desires
& weakness of will.
But the truly evil person, such as you,
actually prefers evil to good.
It's not that you get a thrill out of cruelty:
you coldly & dispassionately want to bring
about outcomes that are bad for other people.

You don't even care particularly if they are good for you.
Mr Hale was merely an excuse
to manifest your life's mission.
Given all this,
it's no wonder that Lorraine rejected you.
She's an intelligent young lady. So, to her
it was all as clear as day.

TURNER: *[properly angry now]* You pathetic little poof.
You're just a … a … little old lady
swatting at a man in a suit of armour with a rolled-up newspaper.
Oooo, you're so outraged ducky. We all despised you,
Franceeeez.
It's you who are a disgrace to the school.
This is a school that trains men & trades in manliness.
Men are rough, can be: should be. We are not
little girls drooling over Gerard Manley Hopkins.
We're not nuns.
You're nothing more than a coward
'at the core', who 'hides behind'
religion & poetry because you aren't
man enough to face the world.
It's too rough for you, isn't it?

& by the way, remember that you're only
the *deputy* chair of the governors.
I have the ear of the Chairman.
His son Rory is a good friend of mine,
one of my wingers in the club.
In fact, I have a business meeting with him
I'm going to be late for. So, toodleoo gents.
I have my way of dealing with all this.

Drake seems strangely satisfied now:
he's finally said what had to be said,
albeit said roughly by his standards
& Turner has revealed himself beautifully.
He turns to Lester:
"Well, off creaks the man in the suit
of tarnished armour … "
waits hopefully for the sympathetic nod.
Lester merely looks depressed.

So, what does Turner do to dispel the bad odour
now surrounding The Gowners (his 'dealing with this')?
Three things.
                    He seeks out the Gowner Glee Club —
four earnest men — & persuades them to station
themselves between the Cathedral & the Central Library
to sing songs sacred & modern before a large red
bucket with the QEH logo … all monies collected
going to charity of course.
                    The Evening Post ignores this;
but *The Western Daily Press* puts it on the front page.

The other two are riskier …
He has some of his handy thugs dress up as Teds —
complications here as some of them *are* more or less
Teds — & be seen to engage in acts of vandalism.
Sometimes these come off.   The hanging
of knickers from the statue of Edward Colson
& the covering of his face & hands with condoms did not.
                    Unsuccessful too was having
some handies paint graffiti under cover of darkness
that was obscene & directed at certain Councillors
& signed 'Your local Modernists.'

Now comes Turner's good luck, to make sense of which
I need to deal with the rivalry between *The Evening Post*
& *The Western Daily Press*. The *Post* is dominant,
but the *Press* has a growing readership & it happens
to have a columnist who is a friend of the Turner family —
name of Camilla Stagg.
Her column exclaims 'Camilla!'
It gives her acid 'takes' on this & that,
always trenchant, hardly leavened by
her laboured wit. Often, they centre around
an anecdote (a bus conductor is not happy being
presented with her £5 note for a two-penny fare: *Why?!*;

the fox she likes that lives in her garden
disturbs the local cats: *And why not!?*).
There is always a stern moral to be drawn.

The photo beside her by-line is of a person —
conceivably a woman — with short brushed-high hair & horn-rims.
The smile is sharky. The eyes penetrate. She also
does an occasional outward-bound column: walking in the
Cotswolds, the Mendips, the Quantocks; striding
the coastal path from Clevedon to Portishead in,
she claimed, a record-breaking time. Photos show her
prop-forward body in big boots & shorts, one foot on a
rock, her gaze saying 'my goal is far from here'.

Many would diagnose an undercurrent
of anger. What is she angry about?
She's not particularly angry: it's just her 'take'
on toughness. She wants to be a gal who's
as tough as only a gal can be. She's proud of her image.
One of her anecdotes was about a policeman she'd
taken rudely to task for ignoring some littering.
He called her 'a dangerous girl'. She dubs herself this
with relish.

She's married to Colonel James Stagg (retired) & they live in
a rural idyll in the Chew Valley (West Harptree Village),
gives Toytown names to her baker, butcher,
nearby farmer & her invented anecdotes about them
are horribly misjudged … but she has a loyal following.

Around this time, she pens an opinion piece,
not under the 'Camilla!' heading, that deals with
The Gowners & the attack on Patsy called
'Who are the True Rapists'? She begins
by expressing deep sorrow at the attack in
a bible-quoting style, after which the tone changes.
Is it not too easy, she asks, to 'heap opprobrium'

for this 'dark event' onto the shoulders of the Gowners *alone*?
Indeed, one of them 'may' have been the 'proximal [her readers
tend to have dictionaries] cause' … but wait.
We must restrain ourselves from 'fuelling' this opprobrium
by 'class envy' & 'civic spite'. This passage is weak
& too revealing.
Then, the meat of her matter.
She argues that sexual attacks on women
are, 'at bottom', the result of a 'masculine culture',
perhaps of masculinity itself. Men exploit women in numerous
ways, not just physically (wives are really slaves, etc. etc.) &
in such a 'climate' it is 'hardly surprising' that 'a virile young blade'
perhaps 'in a moment of drunken madness' did something
'untoward' in a cupboard. This is not a reflection 'merely'
of *Gowner* culture.

The focus: 'Let us not forget that Miss Eviades was working as
the "housekeeper" for the Edwins Hale.
Housekeeper?
A euphemism, says the cynic?
Need we silence him? Must we?
More soberly, we can ask whether these two men
could not cook their own spam & chips, sweep
their own scullery floor. What exactly was her role, gentlemen?
In any event, they paid her so poorly she was forced to
take on this menial & demeaning evening job.
Indeed, let us also not forget that Miss Eviades's father
is a senior member of the Teddy Boy fraternity.
Could he not house her himself, his own flesh & blood?'

Essentially, she argues that George, Ed, & Ned constructed
a 'role' for Patsy that made the attack 'well-nigh inevitable'.

Her rousing coda: 'Oh do let us be *intelligent* about this
& move from the tittle-tattle & small change of proximal
causes to consider, assimilate & accommodate the fact

of the dark river of supremacist masculine mores that floods beneath
our feet.
Yes, indeed, even your Dangerous Girl does not feel safe'.

This piece of naked special-pleading was a hit.
'Proximal causes' were spoken of all over ("I know
I was the proximal cause of Haverill's dinner money being stolen sir,
but … um … shouldn't we consider the background … um … *context* … ").
The typical Camilla supporter used to be
an unmarried gym mistress with a double-barrelled name,
but now the army of Camilla-girls includes many
of the liberal intelligentsia — given that she
she'd half-hit-upon some almost truths without meaning to
or even knowing what she was saying. A body of Bristol
women becomes vocal — in the press & in little earnest
'rallies' on the Downs. Every 'Camilla!' column
now carries an 'anecdote' about a case of female
exploitation she's witnessed.
Needless to say, people begin to warm now
towards The Gowners & freeze toward the two men
who'd employed the victim as their 'so-called housekeeper'.

For the first time sales of the *Western Daily Press* outstrip
those of *The Evening Post*. Every time the *Post* expresses
a hit of scepticism about the Camilla wave it haemorrhages readers.

It was is if the women of Bristol are riding horses
while the men are on foot, hangdog.
Then it all changes.
Photographs change it
as surely as an arrow to the heart
will change life expectancy.

The *Post*'s lawyers advised using French
to head off an immediate legal challenge, so
the heading was: *Un Mariage de Raison*?

One (flash) photograph shows what must be a fancy-dress
party. Somebody who is clearly Camilla (she's recognisablefrom the knees
alone) dressed in lederhosen, halter top,
Tyrolean hat sitting with legs wide apart & on her lap
a pretty blonde in a Heidi-style dress. You could call
what Camilla is doing 'fondling' (the other photos
were too explicit for a family newspaper).   The second
photo has been taken in a West Harptree garden, showing
a moustachioed military type sitting in a deckchair, his
right hand holding a pink drink, his left hand on the upper thigh
of a young man standing beside him in swimming trunks.

This is the end of Camilla.
It's certainly not that the public is intolerant
of Lesbian celebrities.
Nancy Spain is not only accepted by most but adored by many.
Her sexuality is a useful butt for comics
& nobody cares that she lives openly with a woman.
But she has genuine wit & gaiety & she can be seen & heard
in the round because
she's a broadcaster as well as a columnist.
She's almost a member of people's broader family.
                    But Camilla … they never hear her voice
(imagining a rasp). All they have are her columns,
which are her high horses.   What more of her
is there?   My God — *this*!

How did all this come about?

From the Victoria Rooms (between the top of Park Street
& Whiteladies Road) along to Clifton Village there runs
a leafy road of substantial late Georgian houses. Easy to miss
is a venue shrouded by high hedges carrying the sign
ROVERS.   Because the sign is in blue & white
people assume some connection to Bristol Rovers
football club; but if so why do 'theatre people' (well,
that type) arrive there late at night?

Because it's a club exclusive to well-healed homosexuals.
Nothing illegal happens — it's just drinks & music — as it's
a gathering place of the like-minded where
they can be themselves.

Ron Runcie (by-line A. R. Runcie) is a ferociously ambitious
journalist on the *Post* who has invaluable contacts among
the membership & who was able, through them,
to get his hands on these juicy photos of the fearsome scribbler.
One day he simply brought three
photographs along to the office of the Editor, Burford Forbes,
with the words: "I think these may help to redress
the balance boss."
                    Forbes broke out into a cold sweat of
euphoria saying naively: "But she's *married* Ron."
Ron laughs & says: "I'll get back to you in a day or so.
Then we can publish photos of wife & hubby at play."
In fact, he already has the West Harptree photograph.

Immediately A. R. Runcie's by-line appears more often.
He has been promoted too.   But the explosion
which raised him up & wrecked her gives rise, like all explosions,
to a still aftermath
in which thoughts are refreshed & reflection forced.

Burford is relaxing back into the wonderful *status quo ante*,
but reflecting too on how Ron had managed to lay his
hands of these gems.   He calls him in.

BURFORD: I know you don't *have* to reveal your sources
to me but you really must be pretty tight with
these posh queers to get your hands on this stuff.

RON: Not personally tight Mr Forbes; but I know people
who are.

BURFORD: Do you have a girlfriend, Ron?

RON: Yes, I do have one: … Miss Elaine Hall, lovely girl.

BURFORD: Never seen you with a lady, but we'll let that pass …
So, how did you get the Stagg snap? It must have involved
a bit of staking out, or maybe another friend of yours
took it. Who's the boy, by the by?

RON: [*rattled & rash*] Oh, only Marky Parker.

BURFORD: *Marky Parker* … I do declare.
I think we understand
each other, Ron. I don't care what you get up to
in your spare time or even what laws you break but what if
some buggers from the *Press* started trailing you & took a shot
of you with a little mincing machine? Well, it will be cue a long
nasty regime of tit-for-tat, bad for all concerned.
Tell you what, I hear *The Bridgwater Bugle* is looking
for a reporter. You'd better apply.
That's it lad, sorry.

So, the arrow that shot Camilla was one of those
boomerang arrows you have to be so careful of.
The fact that Ron Runcie has never been interested in
sex of any kind only makes its point all the crueller.

Twelve: The First & Final Bout

Is courage a virtue?
Not necessarily.
We think it is because we associate it with
upstanding people like Ed. It certainly is
when it means putting your body & self at high risk
in a good cause … but in a *bad* cause too?
Why not?
OK, OK, you'll say there's no reason why
a virtue cannot be attached to a bad person
as if a virtue could be a kind of module that
is hooked onto the mentality of a bastard
& stays unchanged?
Quite possibly, but I'm pressing on regardless.
It would be difficult
to make the case for Turner being a good man,
but he certainly has courage. Yes it is
fuelled by anger in the present case, but what
quality of the moral heart is not leaked into by other qualities?
On which consideration, see above on the thought
that a virtue could be like a 'module'.
Oh shall we leave this now
& just press on?

It has to be said that Turner's courage will be seen
to be in a good cause: to put an end
to the conflict between the Gowners & the Hales.
As others have said to others & some to him,
this is really just between two men, so why
can't they just have it out between them
& be done with it? He agrees.

This will be — he intends — a physical contest
between himself & Ed.   So where does
the 'courage' come in?
Turner is younger & more fleet, but Ed
is a very experienced fighter, extremely strong
& a ruthless opponent.

It's almost 'sweet' that Turner intends to see this
as a fight 'for Lorraine' — as something heraldic.
But, of course, she is a long-lost cause,
if she'd ever been one at all.   In any event
if he wins the contest he will 'claim her back'
while if he loses he'll fold his arms and say 'Hey Ho'.
                    (Well, that's what he thinks now
in the intersect of anger
& having sickened of it all.)

He has plans for how they'll fight, as we shall see.
Meanwhile, he spends five hours a day lifting weights,
punching bags & taking instructions in the noble art
from a retired pro in a gym on the Gloucester Road.
                    So, how did he reach this point?
The crucial event was his going to see Lester.

He apologised thoroughly for his behaviour
at the previous meeting ('but old Drake really does
rub me up the wrong way') & is suddenly
& almost heartbreakingly sincere.

"I'm sorry Lester, but I just can't get over
losing Lolly. I thought she was the girl of my future.
You'd given your blessing & you seemed to think
we were a good match. Then in walks Hale.
I want her back you see — very badly, do I, to be honest.
Have you changed you mind about us … completely?"

"Let me be frank, Martyn.
While you are — how can I put this? —
one of 'our' people, while I know you fairly well
& have grown to like you & had been looking forward
to our two families uniting happily, something inside of me
stalled & gave rise to an uncertainty,
like a premonition of some kind.
Some feeling that things were not quite right,
& I really must stress that this was *before* either of us
ever clapped eyes on Edwin Hale …
As you know, I am a religious man & did accordingly
seek advice from my pastor, who told me that while
a relationship may be almost mandated by externals
(such as family & position), one cannot 'impose
it from the top down. Like a plant, it must
be left to grow. We can only provide the soil, water
& the sunshine of our love. I think, in short,
that Anita & I, & indeed your dad Percy, had been
guilty of hothousing you & Lolly."

Of course, he is not being 'frank' at all.
What he really means is that Lolly did not fancy
Turner one little bit. He blushes when he gets to
the reference to 'the pastor'. Turner notes this,
feels the old irritation at the Latimer waffle.
He is intelligent enough to see through to what
Lester really means. 'The lightheadedness that comes
from despair' is a fine expressive cliché & when
mixed with a strong directionless anger
you have what drove
Turner's decision-making during those moments.

There is a long silence, during which Lester rings down
for coffee. The coffee comes & Turner asks:

"Will there be a boxing booth at the Goram?"

"Oh yes.
Ed isn't keen & neither am I, but it's the kind of thing
people expect … Yes, that & all those other dubious attractions."

Time now to say some words about the Goram Fair before
we return to Turner & his plans.

Goram Fair is more Thomas Hardy than Enid Blyton.
It's a place where you can imagine life-channelling decisions
being made by desperate men in a hubbub of loud fun.
The 'kiddies' are accommodated but many adults come
for the rough adult pleasures it affords:
a stripper tent (the guy at the entrance, far from being vigilant
against schoolboys, drops his voice between his
'Come on gents, the wife won't mind'
to target & intone to schoolboys 'Fannies & all lads');
a huge beer tent; the boxing booth, of course; in addition to
the fairly innocuous rifle range with its fluffy prizes
there is a highly nocuous one with weapons that can kill
men. The men who take your money on the rides are not
Teds as urban dandies: they are Teds as brigands, so
you *will* be short-changed & if you complain too strongly
you *will* be duffed up. The rides don't jingle-jangle
but blast Little Richard at ear-splitting volume.

The giant … It's imposing but scary
because of its combination of size & face.
It vocalizes Fee Fi Fo Fum or Ho Ho Ho suddenly,
so kids nearby run & hide. To the sensitive it inspires awe.
To some it's a sensory bully.

That said, there are memorable elements you'll rarely
find elsewhere: Cossacks,
who dance their famous dance, perform amazing feats
on horseback with or without swords;
at least one Hollywood cowboy, so B-feature you'll never
have heard of him but there he is with
his real American accent, tolerance, charm,
& chat-up lines.

As for the boxing booth, usually there are four
professionals advertising themselves at the front —
hammering punch-balls into the rickety ceiling.
The idea is that for £1& 6/- you get the chance
to go three rounds with one of them & if you
get through to the end you win £10.
Of course, after a session in the beer tent a tough-guy's
mates will egg him on, will pay the £1 & 6/- for him
so he'll have little choice, less than they have
in seeing him being beaten up in the first round
or toyed with then knocked out solidly. Some do last the three,
but most go in feeling like Freddie Mills & come out feeling
like Poor Poll. All this back-grounded
by the 'Fee Fi Fo Fum' of the looming
giant on the sylvan horizon.

Yes, the fair is exciting, in its way.

As the booth is not in use all the time Turner's idea
is that — how could Ed refuse? — he & Ed will have
a public bout while the boxers 'break for lunch'.
That is, fraternise with some strippers over
a bottle of *Johnnie Walker*.

After Turner has told Lester his idea,
with a new determined hesitancy, Lester
is dismayed. He looks at him & sees his distinctive
profile flattened & red.
He's seen what Ed can lift, how he can intimidate,
he knows his military history. To labour the point:
Turner is strong & tall, but thin & bony; & from the side
his large triangle of a nose simply invites punching.

"Don't worry, Lester. I've got two weeks to get in shape
& learn the noble science. It'll be steak & eggs for breakfast
from now on."

When Lester tells Anita of this she throws down
her head between her legs so her hair scrapes the floor,
utters Noooooooooo at full volume, then takes to her bed.

Another woman who takes this badly is
Yootha, Turner's other sister.
(She's not Remplan's wife.)
A Clifton 'personality', mocked but feared:
tall, striking, of her brother's build, with horsey teeth
& blonde hair piled high. Her clear blue eyes can terrify
even when the mouth below is producing a 10-year-old's sentences.
The only alcoholic drinks she touches
are spirits, never drinks wine, takes a hip-flask of brandy with her
everywhere. Never clearly sober, but always in a kind,
of dangerous control.
She is, by the way, the reason
Camilla Stagg was 'a friend of the family'.
Not because she shares Camilla's tastes,
but because she has no interest in men
(though they have it in her).
Her younger brother Martyn is her life.
She is a second mother to him:
a truth-wielding & protective,
though not comforting, mother.

She has met Ed. Found him admiring her
little Fiat on a visit to Anita. He expended
a couple of ounces of his charm on her
& got close enough to smell the brandy.

"OK then, Martyn," she tells him that evening,
"I've got the measure of Hale.
He's not an honourable straight-backed worker-lump:
he's a bulldozer of ambition.
You get in the ring with him
my darling Will-O-the-Wisp with your
air-slicing proboscis & you can say ta-ta

to your teeth & howdie to mild brain damage.
So, your argument is, dear heart,
that you would like the shit beaten out of you
before the scum of Bristol. Is that right?
Do you think you could walk me through
your thinking on this?"

"He's dim Yooth.
Boxing is a science & he's a scrapper.
I tell you what too: I think he's — how shall I put this —
[a Lester impersonation] a half-man with his
blow-waved hair."

"No, he's not you fool.
He spent two-thirds of the time chatting to me
ogling my tits. & why are you so obsessed by
men being bent? It's disturbing, Martyn, I can tell you."

"& I can tell you to please back off,
mind your own."

"Sorry, old sport, I'm going to do the opposite of that.
I'm planning a walking tour of the Village
& its environs tomorrow.
So, I can call in to see some of your beloved Gowners
to tell them to knock some sense into you before Hale does.
Look Mart, there is only one of him
& countless many of your dressing-gowned weirdos.
Do you think they want a President — *President!* — last seen
being carried to the First Aid tent crying
'Did I win mummy?' through his snot?
Organise, dispose of, then move on.
No symbolic boxing bollocks please."

In fact, it's more of a dodgem-car circuit
than a 'walking tour'. The little Fiat, powder-blue
& cream like the tin of a popular brand of fruit pastilles

ranges & swerves, parks spontaneously on pavements,
blocking drives, in playgrounds. It is certainly unsettling to see Yootha
unfold her long limbs from the pastille box like something
emerging from a chrysalis.

She makes for the front door as if she's rescuing a child
from a burning building & before the door-openers can open their mouths
they hear:
"Toby/Roly/Jasper/Valentine/etc. in? … No? Well find him.
… Oh, that is so WET … Just tell him that my brother, Martyn,
is about to have the shit kicked out of him by that lout Ed Hale.
Tell him to pull his finger out of his arse & phone me soonest.
I'm — "
"I know who you are, thank-you."

Sometimes the targets do not see her coming
& the Gowner is 'at home'.
On one such occasion something sweetly misfires in Yootha's brain
& the following results:

"I tell you what Selwyn. I was looking at some cats
on your lawn just now.
There was a lovely little black kitten being menaced
by a big nasty tom.
& what should happen, but lots of other little black kittens
crowed along & massed & scared the tom away.
I won't spell it out for you. Do it!"

The following is a more typical example of her style
of diplomacy. The scene is an intimidatingly chic
estate agent's office in the heart of Clifton Village
where a young couple are being persuaded to put in an offer
for a hard-to-shift property by prominent Gowner &
partner in the company Brendan Bradley.

"Ah Yootha! How lovely to see you again. I — "

"You know what a silly-bollocks my brother
can be sometimes, Brendan? Well, he's only going
to box Ed Hale in some symbolic show-down crap.
He'll be pulp by the end & not at all symbolically.
You need to get together with the other
Gownee-boys & tell him to stop."

" … I … Do you mind if I first finish up with these clients — "

"*Clients*! Look at Mister who's just extracted a big bogie
with his posh new handkerchief & is looking forward
to examining it later. They can't afford … Where is it?
Royal York Crescent! Tell them to trot back to Bedminster.
& do as I ask. Get on the blower now!"

Despite Yootha's 'refreshing directness' (an early school report)
the approached Gowners do see her point. They do indeed
phone one another; but they do nothing.   Meanwhile,

Ed would dearly love to be doing nothing himself.
                    All is more or less in place for the fair &
he has that feeling of achievement seeping in — till news
of the boxing bout comes. He would rather escape somewhere
for 12 rounds of inaction.   Of course he'll win it.
But, even if it leads Turner & The Gowners to melt away
from him & Ned, this is as tacky a denouement as you could wish.
He's far more comfortable with the odds being against him.

If only Yootha knew Ed's state of mind
she would have offered him a large chunk of
her considerable estate to clear off.
Instead, she thinks this: 'Ed will have to be handicapped
& I'm the gal to do it'.

She tells her assistant-cum-housekeeper to make
one of those turbans for her that she's seen working-class
women wear in plays on the TV, & tells her to get hold

of clear-glass spectacles in the style of those worn
by *Dally Mirror* columnist Marge Proops.
She will wear no make-up — instead of her usual tonne
of it. She is practising her Bristolian with
"Oi firgot me loaf a Lyons' sloiced," being her
'how now brown cow'.
She is torn between a small anvil
& a cobbler's last, opting for the latter in the end
"It'll do as long as he's not in his garden boots."

The door-bell rings around tea-time & Ed
answers it — 'Hooray, he's in his tartan slippers',
thinks Yootha.

"Dilerrrray fir Missur Ell"

She (now wearing brown dungarees) has
wrapped it in brown paper & added
some cotton wool to disguise the shape.
Ed's first thought is that it's an early
birthday present from Vera — it does happen.

"Oh thanks. I'll just —"

"Whoops-a-daisy sir. Shall oi call
an ambliunce or not sir?"

"Hell! My son's here. Just bugger off you idiot."

The big toe is broken, and some of the others
sprained; most toes are in splints & right now Ed
is failing to enjoy the leisure he's longed for.

During the day he walks not far with a stick, fancying
he can still out-fight Turner … all being well —
probably.
The phone rings.

"Dahrling! How ARE you?"

He explains his predicament.

"Ex-act-ly! I had a feeling all was not well.
Call it *Das Intuissimus der Mutter* as the Krauts
call it.
Look dahrling: do not repine.
The solution is just down the road
in the smoky caves of old Vince.
I know he royally ballsed up these gown-burning
devices; but all the more reason he'll want to
make amends & you a lovely SURGICAL BOOT —
I say that's a what they call *zeugma* dahrling;
you see I'm still educating you —
so you can strut about the site of the
Gor-blimey fair as well as
have a triumphant time with the old fisticuffs.
So there you have it boxer-bottom. Only
rang to check in & spurt some balm in your eye.
Sorry, bit scatty today. Must dash. Love muchly!"

Vince! Of course.
That most versatile of engineer-smokers
is only too happy to come over & measure up
& get to his drawing board & then construct something
from a mixture of cardboard, upholsterer's foam,
patent leather, rubber, all scaffolded by what
used to be wire coat-hangers.
He has been wracked with guilt about
the failed mantises, tries to persuade Ed,
between numerous apologies, to try out his new
fool-proof model (the flame won't work unless
the foam does …)
It's a very pleasant afternoon they spend together
& when he delivers the boot pure euphoria is delivered too.
It works a treat.

Ed has had a bout of having odds against him so now
he feels his old self.

Excellent for him; tragic for Anita.
She & Yootha had had a number of sessions
celebrating 'the accident', usually over a bottle
of lighter-fuel-style Bulgarian vodka from a company
Yootha has shares in …
"It's all coming up roses, Yooth. Cheerio!"

Anita is a late riser. One morning
she tugs open her heavy curtains to see
Ed not walking but *running* up the steps to his office.
She spots the boot & gets the picture.
No histrionics this time. Turning pale & still
is what she does.   She selects four sheets
of writing paper & immediately pens four identical
suicide notes: one for Lolly, one for Lester, one for
the dining-room table, & one for Yootha: so there can
be no doubt.

            In these notes she aims for dignity
& hits her usual tone instead. She explains how her life
has been spent 'in a long dark tunnel longing for a son,
I can find simpatico'. 'Mar-Mar' arrives on the scene
& she sees in him the son she has always craved.
The tunnel opened into 'a sunny field off flowers' when
the engagement with Lolly was announced. But now
she must watch a revived Ed 'smashes his dear nose
like a hammer attacks a tomato'. Oh, this humiliation for her
beloved (*not at all maternally* of course) Mar-Mar!
It's too much.
She cannot go on. She is weak
with emotion, but
'Goodbye & all the best anyway'.
She ends with a French quotation that she
translates for them with thorough inaccuracy as:
'A well-placed poisoned thimble can drown a fine peacock'.

Lolly shows the note to her father saying:
"Mummy is pretending to kill herself again."

The previous non-attempts
were variously inspired:
Lolly wanting to go to the Bristol School of Art &
not Benenden; Lester cutting her allowance;
finding grey hairs; turning 60; of course
the liaison between Ed & Lolly; & many more.
(even Labour gains in local elections).
Each time she would take enough aspirin to make herself sick
(each time there's the accompanying hearing loss);
then after that all would be well for a few weeks.
But this time, the hammer-tomato image before her eyes,
she wants to do something with greater 'oomph'.

One idea is to approach the Suspension Bridge
with the obvious intent of throwing herself off —
having waited to ensure there is a bobby nearby.
But given the trouble she'd caused the constabulary after
her Whiteladies Road booze-orgy, she feels they
would be happy to let her jump.

So, instead of the aspirin, she decides to rummage
in the bathroom cabinet & swallow a sample
of whatever is to hand in addition to the aspirin —
Lester's blood-pressure & heart medications,
antihistamines, vitamins etc. — in the hope that
this would be enough for her to need hospitalisation.
The plan, then, is to spread herself at the foot of her bed
surrounded by pill boxes.   She summons
Ophelia's spirit, she wears something long white & chaste,
she cannot settle because of the rumbling in her tummy.
She has taken laxatives. She ends up sitting for hours
in her *en suite* loo feeling desperately faint due to low
blood pressure, a sorry sight she tries to hide
from the world, & fails.

This time husband & daughter feel strong pity for her,
seeing now a little old lady where there had been a harridan.
After this, the old Anita stays dead.

The fair is now underway.

Ed finds he does not like 'show people' very much.
He's happy with their roughness but he can't trust them
& hates the pride they take in their slyness.
The Cossacks he certainly takes to, not Russian most of them
(Ukrainian & Polish often) but a wonderful blend
of artist & warrior. He knows their displays will be
the double highlight of each day & that people will
come just to see them dance, ride & wield swords.

He finds a friend in Micky Israel —
real name of the B-feature cowboy 'Dale Brandon'.
Poor Micky has nothing to do but hang about
beside his beautiful chestnut mare &
the sandwich-board carrying stills from his films.
He twirls his gun, fires it (powerful caps),
& fields questions from boys like: "what's it like
to shoot somebody?" or "do you know John Wayne?"
or "can I have a go on the horse?"
                    Micky's move West
to Hollywood did not turn out so well
& he misses New York. They discuss
the jazz clubs there.

The boxing blokes are alright, but peeved
that the strippers show more interest in Dale
& the Cossacks then they do in them.
There's uncreative tension galore.

On the first day — the Ed-Turner bout
is on the second — Turner goes up to discuss
the arrangements with the booth 'coordinator',
James 'The Bear' O'Keefe, & to have a general look around.
Unable to sleep, he arrives early   to have

reflection forced upon him
on the stirring site.
How did he find himself in this corner?
Is it because he deserves it, given … ?
Then something arrests his vision & thought.
The morning sun catches the metal rail of the
slide on the helter-skelter so that it looks
as if the tower is trapped in a spiral of fire.
There is reflection in him,
but not quite enough to force an alliterating thought
like this: 'There I am, a hollow tower wrapped
in a fatal force field'. Or that he is
set off from the world by his gold, his wealth.
It makes him see himself as trapped.
Of course he is; but is this all this vision means?
He carries it home.

What of Yootha?
Predictably, she has not given up.
She cannot.
Her final shot at a plan to head off the bout
begins with her disabling her bother's car
so that he must get a taxi tomorrow
up to the fair.
    She asks him as casually as she can (as casual
as a pistol shot) "So … about what time are you planning
to get a cab tomorrow then Mart?"

"Ten sharp."

The next morning when he goes down to the street
for the cab he finds that Yootha's been there
since 9.45, having hired a black Vanden Plass Princess,
a huge false moustache, a chauffeur's peaked cap &
jacket. She calls to him

"Yer's Yer cab mate."

If he had taken the bait she would have driven him to
a field outside Gloucester & locked him in the car for the day.

"Oh, morning Yooth! Don't forget to take
your 'tache off when you come up.
You can arm me to the booth like a good big-sister.
Ahh, here's my taxi. See you just before 1.00. Ciao!"

Lester (still wrapped in thought about whether
he's done the right thing by Martyn & Ed),
lets Turner change into his 'boxing costume'
in his office before heading down to the field.
        Turner has some good-luck trinkets
        on his right forearm which are hidden
beneath the long sleeves of a black t-shirt, worn
over black cyclists' track-shorts, not boxing shorts —
perhaps hoping to present Ed & the world with a raw
muscled silhouette.   Instead,
he looks like a member of an avant garde
expressive-dance troupe.

A loud knock on the door. Yootha.

"Come!" she says.

She has been finishing a flask all morning &
is not in the best of shape.   The crowds
do not part for them so she gives one
continual bark of "Move your fat arses!"

Something misfires within her. She looks up,
left, right, finds herself flailing, thrashing around her head,
swatting something.

"Bats! Bats! They've given me fucking bats!"
She runs off as if pursued by hornet swarm
leaving Turner to his solitary transit.

He mounts the booth & waits for Ed to come.
O'Keefe gloves him up.
When Ed arrives all he does is remove his jacket
& tie & wave to a couple of people in the crowd.
He's gloved up now & ready …

Turner begins his expressive dance
by taking up, what the textbooks might call,
Queensberry position 6B,
then moves into furious action; while for Ed
it's as if he's yet to register the fight
has begun.
Initially, all Turner's punches are aimed at the head;
but Ed, sometimes with his guard down, merely
moves out of their way as if from some minor irritant.
Turner's moves are so well telegraphed that his body blows
can be casually blocked.   This continues
for a bit to occasional shouts of 'Make a fight
of it mate'!

Some of Turner's swings, crosses & jabs have
real power behind them.
& you might think that Ed actually *wants*
to be punched hard or even knocked down
so he can begin from his accustomed position
on the wrong side of the odds … Not so,
not remotely so.

Suddenly & in the space of a fistful of seconds
Turner gains the new or true insight
into the flaming-spiral-round-the-tower epiphany:
the tower is Ed, not himself.
It's immobile, straight & tall, above all, well-earthed.
The spiral is not fire or gold: it's glorious good fortune,
his future triumph blazing. It rings Hale to ensure
all Turner's efforts must fail — with 'must'
the must of fate, not of the will.

                    This 'reading' is stamped in
as Ed, almost as an afterthought, delivers
an upper-cut to the jaw, putting Turner out cold.
The usual bucket
of iced water brings him round in the end,
if not quite to himself, then at least
to a walking talking semblance.

"Let's shake hands Martyn.
Let's go & watch
the Cossacks.
They're on at 2.00."

Turner (who's put trousers on
over his track shorts)
looks at the proffered hand, ignores it,
& slopes off into the crowd.

This crowd presses & it's difficult for Ed
to reach the position he likes to watch
them from — behind the third potato.
To explain:
the culmination of the display is a truly breath-taking
display of equestrian swordsmanship in which
Askold (as Ed knows him to be) rides his
black stallion at full pelt, sword drawn, & slices
off the top half of three large potatoes
stationed like eggs in eggcups on 6-foot stalks.
Hey, this is strange:
he feels the space behind him open then close
turbulently, hears: "Yer, steady on mate!"
Turner has come up behind him.

"Hello Edwina!
Now I can get a proper pop at you.
Take — "

Ed just grabs his wrist saying:

"For God's sake, you need to rest.
Have you gone barmy?"

He then puts him in a head-lock.
As he tightens his grip on the struggling man
the right-hand sleeve of Turner's t-shirt
begins to ride up … up … & up.
First there's revealed a bracelet with little hearts on it.
'Cheesy', thinks Ed.
Then multi-coloured strings of the kind
worn by Indian girls.
Finally, as Turner's struggling intensifies
& Ed grip tightens the sleeve rides up further to show
a necklace, wrapped round double,
in thin brushed steel with glass beads
like electric wine gums. *Patsy's.*

"Right!"

He yanks Turner along to his viewing spot & people
give them space.
Here comes Askold & here comes Ed's flashback
to the eyes of the wall-of-death rider as he approaches the rim.
Do he & Askold make eye contact?
Do they 'understand' each other?

Slice …
one potato two potato three potato …
FOUR
Four is the carotid artery of Turner (after a firm, beautifully-
timed shove) as well as his windpipe &
much more in the way of flesh & sinew.
The crowd shrinks back.
Ed stands in triumph over the mess on the grass,
mess like a landed fish from a red sea.

Look: it's as if he's trying to speak, with each
failed word a gout of blood.
Real blood at last.
Real death at last.

The Roman Empire

It could be left like this.
It has been left like this.
It can't be left like this.

Ed wanted to plead guilty to murder,
being proud of having caused the death.

"Do you want to be hanged then?" said Lolly.
"I certainly don't want to honeymoon with a corpse."

No, she honeymooned with a live Ed in Italy:
he having been given a suspended sentence for manslaughter,
his story — told by others, not by him — having
touched the hearts of the jury.
When Patsy was given her necklace back
& told of Turner's end she quickly began to improve;
& Ned's frequent visits had her
walking back to happiness (*whoopah
oh yeah yeah*).

But this is finally about Ned, not his father.
His dad had of course failed to see his gifts,
but Lester saw them plain — over the chess board
& elsewhere. He persuaded Ned
to take some evening classes,
do a few O Levels.
Lester knew of something called
The South-West Matriculation Scheme
through which talented applicants who'd missed out
on A Levels through poor fortune
could apply to University (Bristol, Exeter, etc.).
The Admissions Tutor would tailor an entrance exam

to the candidate's strengths & mark it too. Guess what?
(You can). The Admissions Tutor happened to be
Dr Vincent Hogan from Engineering.
These 'strengths'?
A peculiar mix, like those symbols on fruit machines
that just pop up:
some algebra; elements of formal logic & some physics;
probability theory (he struggled with basic arithmetic
but could explain Bayesian Theory beautifully
& critique it too).

He got in, gained a brilliant First, went to Cambridge
for his Ph.D. — at the Mathematical Laboratory
which later became the Computer Laboratory.
Ned had fallen amongst his own people. Now
he lived on dry land breathing fresh air.
Yes, he found himself to be a genius at inventing
programing languages to convert digital machine code
(in zeros & ones) into symbolic instructions.

I'll own up …
I don't really understand this stuff.
I was once obliged to do a short course on programming
in binary (hilarious in the way
the Keystone Cops are);
I once floppily tried to learn the language LISP & use it
on a BBC computer, failing to make it put ten words in
alphabetical order.
I'm happy
to believe the human mind-brain has some kind
of machine code (not digital)
& that natural languages are analogous to
high-level programming languages;
& that's about the sum of it.

I also vaguely know that Ned brilliantly superseded
Cambridge's Autocode while still a student.

Then most of you will know of
The Hale Algorithm & The Hale Conjecture
for which he narrowly missed a Nobel.
I could Google energetically & essay this up
or I could make something up
but not today please.
The sun's just come out.

No, of course Ned was not
'responsible for the digital revolution'
any more than Augustus Caesar was 'responsible for
the Roman Empire'.
                    But he was one of those
who made it a fact that you'd better
be able to say & mean:
Civis digitalus sum ...
Otherwise you could well
be permanently thwarted in the cold.

Oh, it's like a school exercise isn't it?
'In what respects is the digital world
like the Roman Empire'? 1,500 words by Friday.
Again, I could essay up some ways.
But, again, not today please, not now.

Just this though ...
Communication now feels like
the shortest distance between two points.
It's efficient, all too efficient
& all too prone to fucking up inhumanly.
Look, I'm not a free spirit;
but I would like to be one.
But how can I be
when I can't walk 100 yards from my house
without my iPhone.
My pass-words belong to Caesar.
It's the rules,

the bloody *regulae.*
They give you a kind of power within a domain,
their domain,
a bullshit power within their *regulae*.
Enough!

A couple of years ago Bristol University
opened a fine building on the Clifton Downs
(funded partly by The Hale Foundation;
Ned is at the Salk Institute in La Jolla now)
in the classical style, of Portland stone,
mainly a conference centre
& called The Edwin Hale Building.

Ned made a moving speech in which
we heard …

" … within my mind
or should that be 'within my central operating space'
[*laughter*] I am not the person after whom
this beautiful building is named.
I am not him at all [*stunned silence*].
For me & I hope for some of you
it is named after my father Ed Hale.
He had the vision to move us
to this part of the world.
Yes, he had some eccentric beliefs &
some weaknesses & fits of mean spiritedness;
but my God he had strengths.
He was my hero.
He was *a* hero.
He always supported me.
Always loved me & acted out of it.
This is his building.
Thank you all & God bless my father, Ed Hale."

The applause was wild & sustained.

So … how to finish this?

I had been toying with the idea reporting to you
that in the front row one of the strongest
applauders with the wettest eyes was
Ned's wife Patsy.
But that's pat & sentimental.
Or I could have played it light
& said that I'll end with the words of
Ed's favourite comedian (Jimmy Wheeler)
& say 'Aye, Aye! That's yer lot'.
That's OK, but a bit crass.

I think I'll just do as Miles Davis once advised
John Coltrane to do
& take just the horn out of my mouth.

The End

www.ingramcontent.com/pod-product-compliance
Lightning Source LLC
Chambersburg PA
CBHW011952150426
43196CB00019B/2916

* 9 7 8 1 9 1 2 2 1 1 9 9 9 *